Tales from the Bedroom Wall

The Life and Times of a Serial Thrill Seeker

Steve Blacknell

Old Treacle Press Ltd. 2025

Old Treacle Press

presents

Tales from the Bedroom Wall

The Life and Times of a Serial Thrill Seeker

This is a memoir. All contents are the recollections of the author and to the best of his memory and knowledge are true. Recollections of others may differ.

ISBN 978-1-9168937-7-1

First published 2025

www.oldtreaclepartnership.com

Contributions by Ariana Proofreading & Quality Management

Digital Prepress Services

This book contains memories of anorexia, bulimia and purging, period-typical language and attitudes, scenes involving alcohol and drug use, bodily functions and death and dying.

For Maggie.

Foreword

by Bill Wyman

I met this young man a good forty years ago and we have remained close friends to the present day, having met for business or socially on far too many occasions to mention.

From the start we were brothers-in-arms, sharing a love for the British humour of Tommy Cooper, and of my late friend Stanley Unwin, who would always refer to me as 'Willie Wymold of the Rolly Stokers' - a title that Steve would later often use for me.

But the greatest comedian we jointly shared from afar and also in his wonderful company was the one and only Spike Milligan.

Steve actually did have what could have been a 'Spike' moment with me, when he somehow managed to climb onto the roofs of houses in the Kings Road and suddenly appeared on Christmas Eve on the flat roof of my office and apartment at No.344 wanting a filmed interview dressed as Santa Clause - which he obviously got.

Another interview was filmed during a serious table-tennis match between us, with the two of us struggling to keep pace with questions and answers between forehand and backhand smashes.

We continue to meet as friends, and our e-mails always leave something to be desired, with Steve writing to me as Algernon or Clive and signing off as Fred. My replies would be addressed to Bert and I would sign off as Tarquin, or the likes.

CHAPTER 1

Two's Company and Three - It's a Cloud!

It was Saturday the thirteenth of July in the year 1985. Live Aid.

Without doubt, the most important event in the thirty-year history of rock & roll.

Like a magnificent dart in the sky – as Concorde roared over the White Cliffs of Dover, there was I leaving behind a moderately successful career as a television presenter and plunging into the unknown. I was on board the world's best-loved aeroplane, representing the BBC, the world's most-respected broadcasting organisation, in the company of one of the world's biggest-selling rock stars.

Phil Collins would be the only performer to perform onstage at Wembley and later the same day, Philadelphia. I had landed the improbable gig of conducting the mid-flight interview.

It would be the highlight of my professional career. It would be visible proof to my parents that it had not been a wasted life, and the opportunity to prove to the world that I was now on the A-List.

Assembled was the greatest ever line-up of international rock talent, which billowed forth from a truly global jukebox: Bowie, Madonna, Dire Straits, McCartney, U2, Elton John, Tina Turner, and Bob Dylan! They were all there; but only two people on that historic day ocean-hopped in order to appear on both sides of the transatlantic TV link-up.

One - a former *'Oliver'* star who was busy forging a solo career, enjoying amazing success with a series of popular ballads at this point from his massive global seller *No Jacket Required.*

The other – a loud, garish, 80s TV personality, in a bright pink shirt straight from Dusty Springfield's trashcan, and enough make-up to out-do the woman herself. And that mullet!

Phillip David Charles Collins had completed his Wembley stint and was ready to ocean-hop and create history.

With an estimated global audience of two billion people sharing the experience - after a few quick words on camera, he and I – Stephen James Blacknell, climbed aboard Concorde on route for Philadelphia as part two of one of the busiest days the former Genesis frontman would have in a long while.

For a moment I felt, at last, I really was quite literally part of the jet set.

As I took my seat, I couldn't help remembering the conversation I'd had with my mum only the day before. "What are you doing tomorrow?" she asked.

"Well, Mum, Phil Collins is going to play two concerts on the same day - one on either side of the Atlantic - and I'm going to go with him - on Concorde."

There was a brief pause, then in a worried tone straight out of Alan Bennett, she asked, "How are you off for pants?"

As Concorde sprinted over Wales and geared up to break the sound barrier, back on the ground in London, Queen were taking to the Wembley stage and proceeded to pull out all the stops for what would be remembered as the performance of that day.

As a certain Farrokh Bulsara and Co. took to the Wembley stage and proceeded in getting 80,000 people to go gaga, five miles up in the air, I was throwing up into a small - albeit well-appointed – supersonic toilet.

For years I had managed to keep my bulimia at arm's length, in fact - three years, nine months and sixteen days.

But amidst the air-conditioned luxury of Concorde, as we went faster than sound itself, something literally brought it all back. Maybe it was the puke inducing sight of the well-lubricated pack of British hacks guzzling vol-au-vents and swilling champagne. But suddenly, I felt a wave of revulsion and found myself wondering: 'what's all this got to do with Live Aid?' Surely, we should all be in begging class?

So up it all came: all the top-class grub... the canapés, cocktail sausages, the vol-au-vents, and down it went, all the gratis bubbly. I grasped the rim, and watched what looked like everything I had ever eaten disappear down the toilet bowl. And then, with the confidence of the seasoned bulimic that I was - returned to the cabin to give Mr Collins a few hints on how to handle a crowd.

Seventeen minutes later, as Queen had conquered the world stage I thought I'd thrown up for the very last time, but with my throat a fiery furnace, it was an ominous beginning to an historic day.

But it was interview time and we clambered into the cockpit to see one of the pilots eating a sandwich – a supersonic sarnie!

I was told by our producer at Wembley to 'say my piece' and after a crackle or two we commenced our chat.

Like me, Phil was a long-time Tony Hancock fan, and without thinking we went into some light-hearted Hancock banter to ease us into this historic broadcast.

Once at JFK, it was a swift transit to the waiting helicopter that would whisk us off into rock'n'roll history.

With heart–a-thumping, I gingerly strapped in, and all I could think of was supping one of the cold beers that sat beneath our legs.

I'd never been in a helicopter before, and I often wondered what it must be like... a nice, gentle rise. But no.

Whoosh!!! There was no time – as time was tight as a duck's behind – not a second to spare. Apocalypse Now. Nought to fraught in nano seconds. Stone me!

One minute on the tarmac, next up in the clouds and awaaaay we went. It was just forty-five minutes later that we landed and, in a flash, found ourselves at the JFK Stadium.

There were just short of 90,000 people in Philly awaiting rock & roll royalty.

Philadelphia's very own jazz / reggae / folk icons, The Hooters, introduced 'Live Aid USA' and so the world got ready to rock.

Backstage, it was madness personified – everywhere you looked there were legends aplenty. But cool hand Phil took it all in his stride and was whisked off to join Led Zeppelin for his second drumming stint of the day, leaving this here big nosed bloke from Dartford dazed and a little confused.

By the time Phil was seated on-stage at his piano, opening with the immortal words "I was in England this afternoon!" as per BBC instructions it was my job to contact my camera crew and do a live link back to the UK with the wonderful Annie Nightingale. But live TV can be a right bugger. When it works there's nothing like it... King of the World. But when things stuff up... you too are stuffed.

"Sorry Steve, camera fault" came the cry.

So that was that – so what now?

I already knew the MTV 'VJ's' (Video Jockeys) and I spent the first few hours sitting by the side of the stage with them watching the action unfold. Not particularly used to flying at 1,350 miles per hour then nigh on shitting myself in the team chopper, I started to wane somewhat, and despite the delights of Santana, Madonna etc. I decided I should head for the sanctity of my hotel before I got caught in the rush and gush that would transpire in the late hours.

Once ensconced in my room I was able to watch the rest in comfort with a bourbon the size of Philly itself. ABC TV had cancelled two channel favourites – 'T.J. Hooker' and 'The Love Boat' to make way for this monumental occasion so it'd better have been good, and indeed top stuff it was.

There were, as always, a few dissenters who thought Phil had been showing off doing the double bubble, but by and large the mission was being hailed as a global treat and that he'd pulled off something special.

Phil's appearance behind the kit with a hurriedly formed Led Zeppelin fared less well with punters and critics – as the band were clearly unrehearsed and Robert Plant's voice lacked its normal drive and grit, but hard to blame the drummer! Harsh indeed and you're only as good as the band you are in.

Phil as ever was the consummate performer, but 'tis true' that his performance was a little anti-climactic. However - Mr Collins was a real gent, a funny man, and a joy to be with that day.

I had long nursed a complete and utter loathing of Bruce Springsteen and, for nigh on 35 years, had always moaned to people – journalists - about how rough he'd been at Philly. It was only in 2020, whilst recording a radio show with my great pal and *Top of The Pops* book collaborator Patrick Humphries, that he informed me that 'The Boss' didn't actually appear at Live Aid. Take a bottle of Jack Daniels, a Concorde lagged brain and a mixed-up 33-year-old twat and fuck only knows what I was looking at that day in Philadelphia.

Although we forfeited our £500 fee to be part of the action, we were well looked after flight wise! And although it wasn't quite as flash as the incoming journey – next day I was plonked in first class in a huge British Airways thingy and out came the obligatory welcoming glass of champagne as soon as my arse hit the seat cushion.

Now aloft amongst the clouds once more… with oncoming jet lag… my mind began to wander.

So, what about me? Well, I knew something was going to happen in my life, but I had no real clue as to what it was, but at the very least I was happy in the knowledge that Mum knew I'd not been working in dirty underwear.

As a never-ending procession of white water-sodden cloud puffs paraded by my window, so I could feel my eyes closing, and in my minds eye could sense the faint aroma of carbon dioxide!

Where the hell was I? A very different cloud was coming towards me. It was a murk more than a mist, and suddenly I was back in 40 Friern Road, SE22 barely a year old! But I could smell that smell - like rotten eggs, I could feel it and it was all so real.

This flight of fancy was weaving strange magic indeed, and pretty soon I was literally up and away in the clouds.

CHAPTER 2

The Early Daze

At the start of December 1952, a cold snap had Londoners frenetically stoking their coal fires to stave off the chill factor, and just a few days later the resulting chimney smoke helped to cover the capital with a layer of yellow-black sulphurous smog resulting in that potent eggy smell that engulfed all and sundry.

As the Great Smog of London bought the city to its knees... killing 12,000 people, Elizabeth Alexandra Mary was crowned Queen of England, I made my first appearance in the world. A world where fewer than one in six people owned a washing machine, milk was 7d a pint and footballers were on £14 a week. Gene Kelly's deft depiction of 1920s Hollywood topped the movie charts and, when baby Blacknell was just six weeks old, the UK's first popular music chart was published with a 25-year-old crooner, Al Martino, topping the pop-tree.

Good timing young Mr Blacknell.

My early years were happily spent in Peckham, London. My parents' love knew no bounds and I wanted for nothing. So far so good.

As Russian astronaut Yuri Gagarin was circling Earth at 187 miles an hour, my brand-new kid sister, Claire, arrived on terra-firma at a slightly slower pace.

Then we moved to Dartford in Kent. Dad had a constant urge to move up the management ladder. An invaluable member of the soft drink Schweppes' community, when offered the gig of Branch Engineer at their Sidcup branch, we all trucked off to what was then, to us, the countryside.

I was soon to attend the Downs Secondary School for Boys.

I was everyone's favourite chump - and plump as a pudding due to my love of school dinners and everyone else's too. Cheese and beetroot pie was my favourite, and everything else on the menu too. I took to it like a duck to wet water, and rather a podgy duck with that surfeit of pie still lodged firmly around my ever-expanding tummy.

I was also getting the taste of the bright lights with leads in school plays which prompted my fascination for all things performing.

It was a hint of things to come, though, that I'd talk my way into great acting roles – then utterly screw them up!

As Father Mole Cricket, in Willis Hall's 'The Royal Astrologer', a meaty role for any 13-year-old would-be thespian, my parents were bemused as the local paper reviewed the first night of the play, giving warm congrats to everyone in the cast, except me! Even the bleeding make-up people got a mention! I was the notable absentee.

Perhaps I should have taken note. It was a taste of things to come.

CHAPTER 3

Top of the Props!

My deep obsession with all things pop started with the Joe Meeks' organ-driven space pioneers, The Tornadoes! A 'with it' instrumental quartet whose 1962 debut hit *Telstar* had hit the top of the charts on both sides of the big ponderosa.

Although their subsequent music was basically the same tune played backwards, all the same I LOVED them!

I'd save my pocket money and eagerly hand over my six shillings and eight pence at the local record shop for seminal gems such as The Barron Knights' *Call Up the Groups* and the like.

Dad bought me a string of singles from the sickly sweet *Have I The Right* by the similarly sickly sweety named Honeycombs, to The Moody Blues' *Go Now* and I loved them all.

At my request, dear Dad had papered my bedroom walls in a bright tangerine colour and I began to stick up pictures of my favourite groups of the day. I was in a zillion fan clubs and would sit for hours and stare at my heroes. The Stones, Amen Corner, the ever-debonair Moody Blues, and that wild and woolly crazy combo, The Who!

I've often thought that rock & roll was invented to create the generation gap but through those formative years my progressive Pater bucked the trend. He was infuriating; He actually *liked* the Rolling Stones!

I would hear him humming along to the hits of the day as he passed my bedroom door. The only way to truly piss him off was to play it so loud he had no recourse but to complain. Job done!

One summer's day I sat outside our semi-detached in dad's beloved Renault Dauphine, as Fluff Freeman's 'Bri-Nylon' tones crackled over the radio.

"And pop pickers, up to number three this week, it's that wild man with the guitar, here's Jimi Hendrix and a bit of... Uhhhh... *Hey Joe.*"

My hair grew several feet. Instant hippy. Just add Hendrix.

My ears now started to prick in the alternative direction of The Mothers of Invention, Captain Beefhart, Pink Floyd, and the magnificent Nirvana - the mysterious duo of Patrick and Alex's *'Rainbow Chaser'*, their singles became a vital part of life as I knew it.

And then there was the Incredible String Band - weird and wonderful psychedelic folksters! I was besotted, totally and utterly consumed with each and every element of their very being; The very reason for being here on Earth.

When I was supposed to be hard at work with homework I would listen instead to their epic mystical masterpiece *'The Hangman's Beautiful Daughter'* twenty times at a go, the air choked with incense smoke. Apprentice hippy at work!

I'd marvel at *'The Minotaur Song'*, quake at *'Koeeoaddi There'*, and wonder just how small amoebas actually could be. That was part and parcel of being a 'String Bander' - stuff which in effect meant fuck all to most people on the planet, but to us it was God's work. If I'd only known what was in store for me, I'd have been in dippy hippy bloody heaven.

While at home I was the perfect peace loving, incense sniffing hippy, at school I revelled in my newfound status as a fat and indiscriminately violent rugby 'prop forward' - that's the big ugly bloke who tussles and torments the other lumps in the scrum.

I became the Downs Secondary School club captain and was soooo proud! I'd later create the 'Downs Old Boys' – a team of ex school chums who still loved a good thrash about and the mountains of booze that inevitably ensued with every game.

I'll never forget a particularly brutal game, one bitterly bleak winter's day in the Kent countryside, where we were treated to a very different kind of celebratory drink by the winning team.

We, the old boys, were playing away to 'Vigo'... a platoon of former school pupils - drunks and overly over-weights! A motley bunch indeed. Fifteen strong – flab on legs and two teeth apiece.

It was, in truth, a scrappy game - with knocks aplenty and out and out unwarranted violence high on the agenda... and, as always, we were on the large end of a right good thumping. These chaps were much older than us... whiskered, smelly pub animals who like so many played the gentle art of rugby union for the booze-up afterwards.

Battered, bruised and unamused at the fifty-nine points they'd plundered to our pathetic five, I led our battered heroes back to the 'dressing room', a disused chicken shed, to assess another grinding defeat.

"Excuse me, mate?" came a cry from outside. It was the opposing captain... "Thanks for the game... yeah... sorry it was a bit bruisy... anyway, we clubbed together and thought you might like this... some home-made cider... on us!!"

He produced a large glass bottle and handed it to my team mate Mark who took a sip and with a shrug handed it to me whereby I took a huge gulp! The taste was warm, slightly sweet with an unfamiliar aftertaste that nestled in the throat. I turned to thank my opposite number who was now... gone!

"That's some fucking weird cider is that!" said Mark... and as the words left his lips – so mine began to curl as I realised we had been drinking human piss.

"YOU BASTARDS!" I yelled as I ran outside to see the entire Vigo team falling over themselves with laughter.

"CLUBBED TOGETHER? You sods!"

To this day every time I drink some bad wine, I still refer to it as "Slightly better than human pee." And, when someone blurts... "Oh right... and you know what that tastes like do you?" I just say, "Yes, I do!"

Then I made the move to Mick Jagger's old boyhood haunt, Dartford Grammar School – I couldn't believe one of the old boys was one of my heroes up there on the bedroom wall!

Jagger no less – and I even had his hand me down Geography book!

Ostensibly there to do my A levels, the real reason was despite and because of my bulk I had actually turned into a half decent player. The school had quite a reputation for breeding players of note, and it appeared I had all the right bits to carry me to international sporting stardom! But verily it all fell flat as a witch's tit and so, after two years and two narrow scrape grades in English Lit and Geography, I was left to ponder; What the hell was this long-haired violent peace-loving chappie going to do with his life??

So, what about a being a Radio One DJ, or getting into the BBC doing pop shows? Bus driver? Teacher? Deep inside I knew whatever path I took it would have to exorcise the swash and buckle that lay dormant within.

By now the bedroom wall was layers thick in musical heroes, the orange virtually obliterated by posters and flyers.

I wrote thirty-two letters to figures of the day, from the flamingo-like nose-picking flautist Ian Anderson to Ringo Starr, pleading for advice on how to get into the 'biz'. The only reply came from a certain DJ, Mr John Ravenscroft, aka John Peel who advised me to try hospital radio, which I duly did.

I became the breakfast DJ at St Thomas's Hospital in London for a year – supported by a certain 'Whispering' Bob Harris who was a wonderful driving force in getting my brain in gear, who enjoyed giving young hopefuls the benefit of his experience.

I adored being a DJ. I was cracking bad jokes, playing crap records and taping each and every magical minute I was 'on air'. I had business cards printed – '*Steve Blacknell – Breakfast DJ'* boldly emblazoned in turd brown on an off-white oversized piece of card. I thought I was the bee's bollocks.

I was brought tumbling to the ground some eight months later when I discovered I'd been broadcasting to five deaf wards, and the only people who'd ever heard me were the Matrons and the sodding cleaners.

It was time to move on to pastures anew and put off world domination for a bit. Something different… away from the everyday, dramatic… risky.

It came gift wrapped, one pissed night in the local boozer. A friend of mine had just joined the nursing ranks in the local death-dungeon; Joyce Green Hospital. That's it! I thought, 'that's a bit edgy… I'm in!'.

CHAPTER 4

Nursing and Running Out of Patients

With badly tied back hippy hair, I finally joined a slew of other A-level dropouts as a student nurse, and I ended up working in the 'Psychogeriatric' unit. This rather grand term was in fact a cover for over-full wards of poor, lost elderly men who were delicately termed 'social cases'. In other words, folk with nowhere to go. Bed space was the plague of the day, (no change there) and the turnover would vary from week to week. The constant pressure to get patients home, and away, was inescapable for the duty staff, and it would lead to somewhat dramatic measures.

Mr George Phillips had been in ward H2 for about four months. He was a gentle, small, bespectacled soul, just lying there day in day out, unable to move or even speak. Every day his wife would dutifully sit by his side, reading a newspaper or knitting as he snoozed motionless, only just aware of her presence.

One day the S.E.N, State Enrolled Nurse, my immediate boss who shall be nameless called me into Mr Phillips' cubicle. It was 8am. "Okay, Nurse Blacknell," he whispered, "we're going to give Mr Phillips a vitamin injection that might perk him up a bit." Not that little George could have heard him – still as stone and dead to the world. Being a student, I was not allowed to give 'jabs' but could assist in finding the correct quadrant on the patient's buttocks. Duty done, I returned to my daily bum washing duties – looking forward to the mid-morning coffee and a stale cheese roll.

Around 10am I was passing Mr Phillips' cubicle and I could hardly believe my eyes – there he was sitting up in bed, eyes like saucers.

"Are you okay George?" I asked. "Why yess," came the unexpectedly excitable reply – he was sat bolt upright, eyes bright and a fixed grin.

"Do you think I could have some milk?"

I hadn't heard him speak since the day he was admitted and was in total shock! I dutifully fetched a beaker of milky white, which he duly sipped.

"My Lordy," he cried, "that's amazing." Still shocked I left him and returned to check some 20 minutes later.

He lay motionless, glassed eyes fixed to the ceiling.

He was dead.

His wife came in later that day and was duly informed her husband had died of *pneumonia.*

About three weeks later, one Sunday morning, the ward's big boss called us into his office.

"I just want to say this, and I'll say it just once," he said sternly. "On NO account are you ever to talk to the press about the goings on here. Is that VERY clear?"

So, what we were doing was killing the patients off – those who had no chance of making it home were taking up very valuable bed space. I've never, ever forgotten dear George Phillips. I'm convinced to this very day that it still goes on.

The one thing about nursing back then – and I suspect nothing has changed – is that you have to harden up. It's imperative so you don't go bananas. Very often we would have bets on who was going to die first. The winner would be bought drinks all night. It sounds awful but it's just a fact.

But as a nurse, the golden rule is you do NOT get emotionally involved.

I made that fatal mistake with a little old man, Harry James, who I'd taken to. He was sweetness itself. Each day I'd pop in to make sure he was okay and make him my last visit of the shift. He eventually passed away one morning and I thought: 'Well, that's life...'

Unable to sleep later that night, I got up for some water and as I turned the kitchen light on, I saw him, there – sitting at our table!

I screamed and ran back to the sanctity of my bed and shivered for hours.

It had been a monumental delayed reaction. It was all too much for my battered brain. Just like the wheels on a stagecoach or indeed the spinning Earth itself – my mind had been going so damn fast – time had literally stood still, and it had hit me later... big time!

Never again did I get close to a patient. I had learned my lesson.

It was indeed regular and an accepted practice that one of us would offer a diversion to warn the usually and unusually plump Matron away to one corner of the ward, whilst another would nick the keys to the office drawer to the hallowed 'DDA' drugs of dependence cupboard and hurriedly fill a pocket or two with the golden chalice of medicated goo: Diazepam, or Valium as they are more commonly known. A much-favoured snoozer that would calm the most savage of gnarly beasts. They came and still do, I'm reliably told, ahem... in white 2mg, yellow 5mg and the highly sought after blues, 10mg. I still have a white one in my wallet in case I get one of my dreaded panic attacks – which I do get from time to time.

After stuffing a few lifeless apertures with cotton wool and tying the odd flaccid penis with a bandage in order to get the lifeless ready for the morgue, a gob full of pills and a few pints of strong cider in the pub did the job perfectly. Instant relief! It did indeed seem totally okay – and quite normal. I'll never forget the sight of my fellow nurse, Del, pushing a trolley up and down the ward, tripping on LSD ringing a bell and shouting, "Bring out your dead!" at the top of his voice.

You HAD to be hard!

On the subject of hardness, and somewhat late to the starting blocks at nineteen years old, I lost my virginity one steamy August evening, on a spare bed in Ward 21 of the West Wing, to my Jamaican sexpot staff nurse. She plied me with goat curry and huge glasses of rum. When I was done, she threw me off her like a sack of spuds, washed her hands and floated away. I was in love!

Until that is I discovered she'd not only shagged most of the students but also the domestic workers and some of the patients too.

But within a few weeks, 'love' had turned to lust everlasting and I'd begun a quite meaningful relationship with Sheila, the staff shagger as she was known.

In actual fact she had started to fall for me a bit and, as a clueless dippy hippy peacenik, I didn't quite know what to make of this big, black temptress fawning over me.

She gave me a picture of her lying scantily clad on a huge bed – which I delighted in showing my Nan and Grandad at Christmas just after lunch.

Now, after five-ish decades in the music business I can confidently state, I saw more sex and drugs in those hospital days than in the daze of the music industry. It was a hazy, crazy time. And, in its way, a perfectly reasonable rehearsal for the idiot madness that was yet to come.

I'd been having rambling drunken evenings with three chums - Pedro – a mysterious cloaked bulge of a man, a wiry haired speed freak called John... and 'Kof'... a spindly eccentric who I'd met at school.

We were all bored shitless.

With just three weeks to go before I was to qualify to be a real-life nurse, the four of us met in our local and decided enough was enough. We were young, daft and wanted to explore life a little.

Next day I said bye-bye to a teary Sheila, and literally walked out of my job.

CHAPTER 5

Go West Young Man!

We decided that sunny Cornwall was about as far away as we could get, and eventually the day came as we assembled outside my house. There were the three of us stuffed into a Hillman Imp... along with a motley array of loaned household appliances and a glove compartment rammed to the gills with black microdot LSD tablets.

And there was Pedro – astride his beloved imitation Harley Davidson. A sight indeed.

"Bye-bye all," I shouted to my teary family and, "See you when I see you!"

How COULD I have said that? Ah, the disparity of YOOF!

We had two aims in mind: To get a job in the land of opportunity and take as many drugs as we could without killing ourselves. That wish nearly came true for yours truly on that fateful fifteen-hour trek.

We all took turns to get on the bike with the big man.

I'd never been on a motorbike before – so when we'd stopped around midnight – just over the Tamar Bridge – I yelled to Ped, "Okay twat-face let me on... I wanna try this!" and climbed gingerly on the back of the mobile lump of metal.

It was only whilst hurtling down a dreary dark A-road half an hour later that I noticed Ped's helmeted head start to droop.

He was falling asleep.

I could just make out a big bend ahead.

"PED... FUCKING WAKE UP!" I yelled, just in time to see his head raise, as the rusty brakes screeched into the night. That was nearly the finish before we'd even started!

After a few weeks camping out in the seaside towns of Perranporth and St Austell, we came upon a little cottage in a pokily cute hamlet called Ponsanooth, midway between Redruth and Falmouth. It was hidden away at the end of a lazily long drive behind a clutch of ageing trees. It was everything we'd dreamed of. Steve Winwood's band, Traffic, had locked themselves away in a Berkshire cottage to write their seminal debut album *'Mr Fantasy'* in 1967, and somehow, we felt we were emulating that whole hippy ideal. Four blokes out to get out of it and enjoy every moment. We were on a Mission!

But, of course, we had to work. Pedro opted for the local pursuit of tin mining!!! whilst John, Kof and I went for the more sedate option of child care and nursing.

'I wonder if any of them have a DDA cabinet', I mused.

My first gig was at Tehidy TB Hospital, where I bagged the worst job of the lot: phlegm collecting! My job was to walk up and down the chest unit, or whatever they called it, and offer the spit tray to whoever felt like relieving themselves of whatever muck was hanging around their upper tracts.

Back in my hospital routine, where drugs always seemed to help time go by, I took to dropping a microdot whilst hitching to work. This was indeed a revelation as, by the time I'd donned my white uniform and tied my hair back, I was completely off it.

So out they poured... waterfalls of rainbow coloured mucus into my white plastic tray. I'd often think I was in a dragon's den with all these multi-coloured flames jetting out into my secret pouch.

It was only when I'd come down a bit later at the cottage that it would occur to me what I'd been doing.

In fact, the LSD we'd scored was very 'heavy shit' indeed. On one particular visit to Penzance aboard his Harley, Ped and I were tripping with him yelling like a twat the entire journey. All four of us were convinced there was a colony of 'mint-men' living in the grounds of the cottage. They were little stick men who lived in a big nest. I had no idea, however, that they had a colony in Penzance... and it was only when we were both atop a particularly threatening cliff top that I decided that I could fly.

I could imagine myself fluttering my arms as I dropped deftly onto the sand below. I must have been ten feet from the edge when Ped yelled out "Oooooh look, a mint nest!" In an instant I was with him. There was Mr Mint, Mrs Mint and a whole straggle of Mint Juniors, little stick people crying to us to help them.

Back in the cottage later and 'coming down' nicely, it suddenly occurred to me how near to the edge I'd actually been. "Stone me," I cried, "Mint men!"

We often had visitors from Planet Kent, and one such, a towering scruffy long haired lanky lad called Rick, came to stay.

He informed us that he'd been the first person in Britain to be arrested for 'internal' possession of Cannabis!

It transpired he'd just 'scored' a huge dollop of resin, and when he saw a local policeman walking towards him, he'd popped the lot in his gob. When the copper then asked him where he was off to, in a vain attempt to talk, had showered him with a blast of half-eaten bits of dope.

He was promptly arrested and taken to the local nick. We all thought this hysterically funny and celebrated with a joint the size of a small house.

We tripped each and every weekend, taking it in turns to hang out at the farm gate at the bottom of the path.

One sunny morning, Kof and I were perched precariously on the same old gate, completely detached from reality, and everything I said sounded like I was saying 'Eighty-Eight'; even the trees were in the shape of 88! Suddenly I espied a brightly coloured, small figure coming towards us. "It's a fucking Martian!" screamed Kof. And of course it was. "And look," he yelled, "It's got a land mine detector!" Sure enough, this Lincoln green Martian was bearing down on us, holding a bright red mine-detector. "What the hell do we do?"

"I'll handle it... leave it to me," I yelled. Slowly, I baby-stepped towards it. "Excuse me," I stuttered, "Are you real?" Exit one Cornish alien at a speed of knots, and in a flash, it had gone. We couldn't believe our luck and later that night we were full of wonder at just how we'd ended up in an alien zone!

It was three weeks later that I was once more hanging on the gate with Kof, but this time drug free. Suddenly out of the corner of my eye I could see someone or something coming down the hill towards us. It was a neighbour walking her pet dog. It had a red lead and she was wearing a bright yellow jumpsuit. So, imagine you're out for a doggie walk one sunny day and a bloke with a big nose and waist-length hair totters up to you and asks: "Excuse me, are you real?" Great stuff is LSD.

We would go back and forth to Kent from time to time to get our 'supplies' and were never without a tab or two, but we didn't know about the brown acid! These were tiny little pills that packed a punch like Mohammed Ali, very, very strong. It was a few weeks later, on a Saturday night that we all dropped a 'few' brownies. "Gotta be careful, these are strong stuff," yelled John.

The first thing I saw that made me jump was Pedro sitting in a chair with these giant headphones. He looked as if he was on Planet Coo Coo, eyes rolling, deep in brain-talk with Jimi Hendrix's stoned epic '*1983 – A Merman I Should* Be' from the '*Electric Ladyland'* album with the cover infamously decked with nude ladies who he was also ogling at. Totally consumed by the music, he unplugged the headphones and glided across the room... still beating time with the music that wasn't there!

The brown pills had done their work... and he disappeared into the toilet where he sat, singing amidst loud farting noises, plops and the sound of splashing for what seemed like an eternity. His fat frame would eventually emerge – and as the door burst open so too THE most unpleasant, putrid smell pervaded the entire cottage. He headed straight for the kitchen without a thought for the wash basin and started making what would become his trademark LSD Super-snack... a beef dripping sandwich made with the lard bit coated in tomato sauce.

He also delighted mid-trip saying goodnight to us all – waving as he climbed the stairs. What seemed hours later there was a loud knock at the door. Once open, he'd roared in... astride his bike, be-goggled, headphones ensconced outside his helmet, headlights blazing – straight into the living room.

Somehow our fat friend had shinned down the outside drainpipe in an attempt to freak us out. It worked. We screamed and shouted in horror as he pissed himself rigid. Great times!

One ghastly last bad trip at the cottage involved eight feet tall Mint Men coming at me with hatchets... and that was it for me.

Those were wonderful days but they had to end, and by the Spring of '72 I was back in the safety of 35 Berkeley Crescent, Dartford, Kent.

You'd think I would have learned my lessons with the trippier side of life... but... no.

Now cozily home, I'd often take a day out with my beloved Sooty puppet and drop some acid.

One such day I nipped out and dropped a tab of the highly intense black microdot - a particularly potent little bugger that would ease you away from reality into another time and space in thirty to forty magical minutes. I loved it. But the trouble with LSD is that you should be in a safe environment – yet my buccaneering forays still bore a fatal attraction. After being out all day – and convinced I had come down sufficiently – I ambled back home to be met at the front door by my dad, "Hello son," he said, as one would. As I gazed at him, I could clearly see he was raising an axe at me, about to strike.

"SOD OFF, leave me alone!" I screamed and ran to my room, slamming the door and diving under my bed.

Years later one Christmas I explained to him what had happened. "Yes," he murmured, "I thought something was up. And I'm not THAT thick son."

CHAPTER 6

The Silver Lady and Other Hairy Moments

The Tenth National Jazz and Blues Festival was held between the sixth and ninth of August 1970 at The Plumpton Racecourse in East Sussex.

A somewhat slimmer and sprightly revved up eighteen-year-old, my application to become a full time Hippie was in the post.

I had tickets to see Jimi Hendrix himself at The Isle of Wight Festival on the 26th – but I thought I'd break myself in at Plumpton and get the 'vibe' of what I was meant to be and what I was meant to do to fit into this exciting new scene. My Dave Clark days were but a monophonic memory and I was now ready!

Raring to go, I told Mum and Dad not to worry and that I was a big boy now!

Once there I met up with a few chums and meandered about the fields – happy to be hippie! Well – half a hippie! My hair was just over my collar and with my wackily patterned oh-so conservative oatmeal shirt and loon pants I'd felt the part, but there I was surrounded by freaks with hair down to their waists smoking drugs!

It was Ginger Baker's Airforce, he the wild man drummer from supergroup, Cream, who were the headliners with an amazing line up in tow.

They were indeed a mighty outfit with Baker at the hub – driving the band with huge gusto, and direct from a residency on my bedroom wall, a certain ex-Moody Blue, Denny Laine, – but I couldn't take my eyes off one of the backing singers. She had long blonde hair down to the ground, a skirt so short it hardly made it as a bloody belt, and long silver boots. I was mesmerised and spent the entire set with eyes firmly fixed on her. I remember her sticking in my mind as 'The Silver Lady'.

Also on the bill were the 'prog rock' ensemble, Steamhammer, also a newly formed supergroup called Judas Jump, featuring ex-Amen Corner saxophone superstar Alan Jones and gasp! The Incredible String Band. Looking back, it's only now that the enormity of that festival hits me like a house brick. I would end up meeting the love of my life through Steamhammer and end up living with members of Judas Jump and the ISB!

Of course – blissfully unaware of what was to materialise in later years I just gaped in awe at these demi-gods, as I lay there surrounded by discarded litter and drowning in the innocence of it all.

It was a landmark event in my young life, and I loved each and every minute.

It was a special day in rock history too as Pink Floyd premiered their new release *'Atom Heart Mother'*, complete with a massive wall of sound that boomed around the park and shook us to the rafters.

It was all topped off by an amazing appearance by the outrageous comedy troupe, The Bonzo Dog Doo Dah Band, fronted by the extraordinary Vivian Stanshall. He performed at the top of a ladder at the side of the stage and in a bid to freak out those 'tripping' in the audience turned up the volume and reverb bellowing, "Hello Wankers" to volume twenty-five. I was smoking a joint that had been given to me and as I struggled to inhale, so the day got very weird indeed.

The Incredibles were exactly that and left me feeling as though I'd found somewhere to belong. Having said that, the whole buccaneering vibe was to fade miserably as I had no money left and had to call my dad to drive down and rescue me.

Tail firmly between my legs I didn't say much on the way back to Dartford, yet banging away in what was left of my brain was that crystal clear image of the silver lady jiving on stage.

The image never left me, and when some eight years later ex-TV cop David Soul topped the UK charts with *'Silver Lady'*, I recall thinking that something was up, but what it was I had no fucking clue.

If only I'd known.

Just one year forth from the infamous 'Woodstock' – a year later the 1970 Isle of Wight festival had a lot to live up to and managed to once more secure the services of a certain Johnny Allen Hendrix, aka 'Jimi', to top the bill. He was joined by a slew of rock icons... The Who, The Doors, Joni Mitchell et al.

No wonder then it lured over 600,000 people to invade an island of just 150 square miles, and yours truly was one of 'em!

Resplendent in my prized black starred T-shirt and slightly longer hair, I was now revelling in the knowledge that something significant was in the air!

When you turned to a fellow reveller, there was no need for words, no need to speak. A smile said it all.

I've not known a feeling like that since.

I was accompanied by my Grammar School chum Dicky D – a towering loud and loony streak of silliness who laughed incessantly and found it hard to take anything remotely seriously. The last thing I heard of him he'd found 'God' somewhere... a lovely chap.

The festival itself was history on grass, in every sense of the word! I wondered where the hell everyone came from, and despite my growing confidence that I was well on the way to being a fully-fledged freak, the truth be told I should have had a bloody L-plate round my neck.

Everywhere there was swirling hair, bare bosoms, a proliferation of naked babies, and the neighbourly niff of the by now familiar dope smoke swirling heavy in the air.

To quote a certain Kiki Dee... I had the music in me, for sure - but still couldn't fit the pieces together.

It was quite dangerous to take drugs into the festival itself... Dick and I successfully hid LSD tablets in dummy toothpaste tubes but were desperate to find some grass to calm us down if the 'trip' went tits up.

Later that day as the hallucinogens were just kicking in; I was squatting outside our tent when I felt a sharp tap on my shoulder... "Hey man... wanna score some hash?"

Turning, I couldn't believe my eyes.

"Ullo Blacknell you bastard!"

It was another school mates' brother, Ricky!

What were the odds? We laughed till we felt sick, and got completely out of it.

I danced like a twat to T Rex's *'Ride A White Swan'* and when, finally, Hendrix took to the early morning stage on August 31st, I was just dumbstruck. There he was ...

He'd been on just thirty minutes when Dick signalled... shall we go? And so we did... we'd seen God in all his glory and that was enough.

In truth, we were all on a road of discovery, and like so many thought the dream would never end.

A bit of digression here...

Who would or could have imagined that just six short years later, the nation would be dodging spittle from the 'hippy haters' aghast at the anger and frustration of a new generation, out to see the system tumble. No change there as the flower generation wanted the same thing... but just wanted to do it with a bit more grace!

As mentioned, your parents were not meant to love your music – it was there for a reason. To divide the adults from their offspring and give both generations something to shout about.

Just as the hippies trod all over the clean-cut look of the early sixties - so punk spat at the peace and love with its manufactured anarchy, and an anger that would ultimately fizz out and give way to yet another fashion flurry in the bizarre shape of mullets, shoulder pads and eye watering colours that defined 'The New Romantics'. One replacing the other, with what was generally the direct opposite of what went before.

Enter Mr Blacknell wearing more make-up than your average stripper and an effeminate look that would define my TV and personal self.

But a final word on the festival before I jump back into the 80s a bit later on.

For many of us, the Isle of Wight Festival remains a beloved bookmark in our formative years.

So often when it's brought up in conversation someone will state, "Yes, I was there!"... "And so was I." says another.

A reminder of the smile that said a thousand words.

CHAPTER 7

Life in a Sausage & Living with Gods 1973

Having turned the grand old age of twenty-one, my wondering wanderlust was kicking in once more – it was time again to leave the family nest, and in a teary farewell I bade bye-bye to my bedroom wall, with my dear Dad saying, "It'll always be there for you son!"

A few of us found a house in a quiet residential place called Barnehurst, near Dartford. It was a pleasant enough semi-detached affair with a nice garden and two bathrooms. For no apparent reason other than the amount of drugs we were now taking, we named it 'Sausage' and put a sign on the front door with a picture of a sausage on it to underline the fact.

Drugs were in good supply and our besuited neighbours thankfully had no real idea what was taking place at number thirty-two Windermere Road - I think they would have been a little upset.

We were 'Stoned in Suburbia' and revelled in that rich, riotous feeling of 'Stuff You!!' Important stuff.

At a loss of what to do next, I became a fire extinguisher salesman, and a good one at that. I would wait until the weather became uncomfortably cold and wet, then I would traipse around the neighbourhood for a while until rain sodden and frozen - then knock on a door. Pity is a wonderful thing, and boy did it pay off. I became the south-east's top salesman and was given a silver cup in a pub in Welling. I sold it two days later to buy some pot.

I soon quit the glamorous world of fire-extinguishers and joined the weary world of unemployment. 'Sausage' life had become rather humdrum.

These were heady times indeed. One of our number, a thin, bony, long haired blonde chap called Ray had read somewhere that to be confined in a space with flashing lights could bring about hallucinations and a general feeling of disorientation.

A few weeks later about 3.30 one Sunday morning the house rocked with the familiar strident chords of Rick Wakeman's, *The Six Wives of Henry The VIII.* Half awake, I made my way down the stairs. Opening the lounge door, I was confronted by a swaying grinning figure, draped in a pair of curtains and walled-in by cardboard boxes, hammering away at an upturned chest of drawers with a battery of flashing beacon lights beaming down on him.

It took him days to recover.

'Sausage' was a haven for the weird and wacky.

One night I'd consumed too much speed and threw up out of the top bedroom window. Minutes later the bell went and standing there was a totally stoned flatmate, Adam, hair thick with sick. "Hey Man, it's raining!" he whispered softly.

'Ooh – I know'... said I to me one sunny Saturday morning. 'I'll drop The String Band a letter. Nothing will happen... but it's worth a bash!' And so – after a little 'livener' I put a shaky pen to paper.

'Dear Incredible String Band' it ran, 'I worship the very ground you walk on and I would like to come and work for you.' The missive was duly dispatched with a second-class stamp and I thought no more of it.

Two weeks later, around 7.30 pm, the Sausage hot line sprang to life. "Oh, hi, yes, it's Malenie here. Mally from the String Band, is that Steve?"

"WHO IS THIS?" I shrieked, "If this is some kind of joke it's not funny!" Came the gentle reply, "This really is Mally. We got your letter the other day and it was wonderful. Would you like to come up to meet us all?"

In shock I slammed the phone down. But it soon started ringing once more. "Hello", said the fairy-like voice. "I think we got cut off, are you there?"

Two weeks later, bursting with excitement and trepidation, I was on a coach bound for Peeblesshire in bonny Scotland. This was like a Catholic nipping over to the Pope's for a swift half. I was going to meet Robin and Mike... The Incredible String Band.

The Row was a string of terraced cottages high in the hills near Innerleithen, about 40 miles from Galashiels. Away from everything. Peace itself.

I sat in cottage number one. Mally was politely going through the tour plans for the latest incarnation of the ISB, an unlikely yet intriguing mix of full-on electric meets eclectic.
In truth this was to be the beginning of the end of the ISB, with Mike fresh from working with The Who on his '*Smiling Men*' solo album, whilst Robin had paid further homage to his Celtic roots with his own platter, '*Myrrh*'. But all I knew then was, I was there, at The Row. The fucking Row!
As I sipped coffee, I saw a head I knew bob past the window. The door opened... and in he came. My jaw hit the floor. "Hi. I'm Robin," he piped.
"I'm, er..." prompt please, "errrrr, oh that's it – erm - Steve."
And so, I met them all. The wily Mike Heron, dashing new recruit, Malcolm Le Maistre, et al.
I was dumbstruck.

I was face to face with some of my bedroom heroes. Two nights later I was told that Robin wanted to see me. I gingerly entered his cottage to find him swaying over a blazing log fire. "Have some of this," he beckoned. It was his own magic brew.

As far as religious experiences went this was pretty much up there. Jesus had just offered Catholic Joe half a Guinness. Extending his wiry frame, he gazed out of the window... and extolled with a sparkly grin... "Long May Your Lum Reech, and Your Peet Fire Hey Drottle... Jumpin' Geordies in Yer Pooch and Wheskey in Yer Bootle!".

Dumbfounded I guzzled my glass, too shaken to speak. Too shattered to know what was going on. What did that all that mean? I didn't care.

What it DID mean was that I was lost in a dream that had come true. If anyone had told me back then in my swotting days, next to my bedroom wall that I'd be there with my hero having a bevvy, I would have said, not in a million years. But - I was.

And it got better! They offered me a job!

It was selling their merchandise on the road with a commission, and my trusty glove puppet Sooty would join me. He came everywhere with me – he never said a bloody word but he was great company.

And so it was that summer's day in 1972 that my dad dropped me off at the Brighton Dome. Good old Dad. That was where the tour was going to start and I was beside myself with anticipation. In awe at the sheer spectacle of what lay ahead.

Susie Watson Taylor was Mike's partner and in charge of touring. It was her I was meant to meet. Pumped and primed, I sat outside waiting for the band to show. "Hey, I'm here."

Her face sagged. "I'm so sorry, Steve, there's been a mistake, and we can't take you with us." My world crumbled.

It turned out there had been an 'admin' screw up at Island, the band's record label. She could see I was in pieces and said, "Take a walk along the shore and come back in an hour."

To contemplate suicide at twenty-two years of age was somewhat dramatic and OTT, but as I gazed at the sea, I felt my short life was over and done with. As I stood there gazing at the water, I heard a voice behind me – it was Susie. "It's alright... it's okay!" she screamed. The relief could have been heard on distant shores. A size ten explosion!

That night I stood nervously front of house at the Dome as not only the ISB's merchandise guy, but in fact, as the meeter and greeter to the adoring flock of fans who had come to see and hear their heroes.

As if to confirm my arrival in the ISB camp, I donned red carpet slippers and a bright silver and green jacket as the backdrop to my navel-length, shiny brown hair. And there was Sooty by my side. We were ready to RUMBLE!

I'd had this infernal glove puppet since I was four years old. Now looking a little bedraggled, he was nevertheless my alter ego and constant companion, and so it seemed right that he should accompany me on this finest of adventures. I was soon seen as a member of the troupe and even had my own little fan club. I was earning well over a hundred pounds a week; a fact that was not lost on Mark, the sound man, who'd joined the band fresh from a successful world tour with Paul bloody McCartney. He was pretty pissed off in truth but did I care? Nay, thrice nay I say!

After the initial dates, we returned to the solace of The Row and it was there one blustery autumn Sunday afternoon that I experienced one of the most bizarre and unforgettable experiences that still haunts me to this very day.

There came a knock on the door. It was the ever-ebullient ginger-bearded drummer, Jack. "Get yer kit on Steve – we're off on a jolly jaunt."

Amongst the rolling hills of Innerleithen and beyond, lay a castle.

It was the property of The Right Honourable the 3rd Baron Glenconner – alias super rich landowner, Colin Tennant, a well-known eccentric and avid socialite. He had purchased the island of Mustique in The Grenadines for the princely sum of £45,000 some fourteen years previously with his wife, the former Lady Anne Coke – who was lady in waiting to the equally flamboyant Princess Margaret.

Apparently, we had all been invited round to theirs for tea and buns!

And so, we marched in line, Robin, Malcolm, Mike and Susie, Malenie, et al, till the castle came into sight. Bearing in mind I was still in cloud cuckoo land – I was barely feeling reality, whatever that was. I was in another world entirely.

Ambling into the grand hall, we were solemnly greeted by a tall skinny servant with a gigantic nose who ushered us toward some huge wooden doors. We could hear glasses clinking and a piano tinkling.

As we gingerly entered, the sight before us was enough to make the bleariest eye sore!

There in the centre of this grandest of gallery rooms was Tennant himself, propped up against the unmistakable figure of a certain Sir Roderick Victor Llewellyn who in turn was slurring over the mystery piano player, a certain Countess of Snowdon – aka HRH Princess Margaret.

"Do come in folks," exclaimed Tennant. "Have a glass of poo!!"

Margaret herself was dressed to the nines in full royal regalia with a ruby red sash over her shoulder. Cigarette dangling precariously from her gob, while the other two frantically tried to keep up with her mumbled but strangely evocative version of the Monty Python classic, *'I've Got a Ferret Sticking Up My Nose'*. Without blinking, we all joined hands and danced frantically around this unlikely trio singing along and laughing so loud it made the walls creak.

So here was I with my Gods. Dancing around HM the Queen's younger sister. It's an image that's never left me.

As stated, one of the String Band's songs had always gripped me to the very core.

It was the thirteen minute psychedelic folk opus, *'A Very Cellular Song*' that appeared on *'The Hangman's Beautiful Daughter'*. I was totally consumed by it and the mysteries that surrounded its reflection on life, love and amoebas! I would spend hour upon hour, pondering over the intricacies and nuances as gimbris and Jew's harps lay deftly alongside harpsichord, piano, guitar and the kitchen sinkipoo!

It was indeed a few weeks after the Margaret incident that Mr Heron himself revealed to me that he'd been tripping on LSD and ripped up a Radio Times and shuffled some of the words together whilst listening to Radio 4 that made up much of the song.

Did I feel robbed? Far from it - I was in seventh – verging on eighth heaven!

In between tours I'd either be at The Row with them or back home in downtown Dartford.

It was a weird but wondrous lifestyle. In truth the ISB never became the force they could have been... but the likes of Dylan, Robert Plant, Bowie, amongst others, have all cited them as major influences and it all could have been so, so different.

The Woodstock Festival had made the careers of a whole host of bands from Santana to Ten Years After and beyond, and there are many tales of those who didn't make the cut of the subsequent movie a year later. The ISB had refused to go on stage during the Friday night folk schedule amidst electrical storms and rain and had subsequently got lodged between the drumming legend Keef Hartley and the boogied blues of Canned Heat on the Saturday and had bombed dramatically.

Keef was a mate in later years and he'd often curse and swear about how he too missed out on the movie. He was one of the many who'd come up through the John Mayall school of rock – and as a drummer and bandleader was the hippy Dave Clark of his day – bald on top – complete with authentic cowboy hat or the occasional Red Indian Headdress!

He was an amazingly funny and engaging man who lived in West London in a house called 'Ayalam'. I recall one drunken day at his gaff asking him just why he called it so and he replied through his bushy moustache spitting beer at me, "It's Malaya backwards." And that was Keef. One of rock's true gents. He died at just sixty-seven years old and is oh so missed.

The ISB remain the ultimate cult band to many, and their songs live on, as indeed they do in my head each and every day.

Thanks to the duelling forces within the band, they eventually imploded in 1974 and I returned to the relative obscurity of Dartford.

They say meeting your heroes can sometimes be a disappointment but to me this had been the ultimate prize!

This was to be the start of meeting my bedroom wall heroes.

CHAPTER 8

Sowing the Seeds of Yukk

See Below

It was the summer of '73 and I'd moved to one of the ultimate hippy outposts, Great Malvern in Worcestershire. I'd befriended a lovely longhaired soft-spoken chap called Phil Webb when I'd visited the town with the ISB some months before, and in need of a job I got a gig at the local special needs home, Dalvington, working with Down's syndrome kids, which I loved. I was fascinated by them and one hazy night Phil and I reflected as we gazed over the town from his hillside flat.

We talked about how they were always smiling and laughing, and they just lived for the next meal, the next walk, the next passer-by to say hi to.

As the ever-obscure Captain Beefhart played softly in the background, it was Phil who remarked, "Maybe it's that theory that says the brain is not a creative force at all. It is, in fact, a shield that blocks out most of what the Universe throws at it. Therefore, as these, supposedly unfortunate, people have a brain defect they are in fact 'blissed out' all of the time. Lost in a sea of total simplistic joy. Maybe WE are the ones who are less fortunate!"

I never forgot that and loved working with my special needs charges even more after that.

Drugs were hard to come by and indeed too expensive for the likes of yours truly. Although I loved my job, the pay put the P into Peanuts, and I could barely afford to eat.

I had befriended another hippy chap, Simon was his name, and he introduced me to the delights of Dodo Asthma tablets. They had a strange speedy edge to them and even though they made one feel nauseous as shit they were cheap and plentiful from our local branch of Boots! The key was, as always, the label. 'Do NOT take with any other cough and cold medicine' it said. So - four Dodo's and a bottle of dizzy drowzy Benylin cough medicine were enough to send you 'off without a cough' as we would say.

Pedro would often come and stay in my tiny flat and we'd venture out on a Wednesday night – stuffed full of pills and liquid and go to see All-In Wrestling at The Malvern Winter Gardens. This wasn't exactly LSD but it did the trick! We marvelled at their muscle and bustle and cheered and booed along with the blue rinsed Malvern Lady wrinklies who were nearly wetting themselves with bile and anger at the heavyweight ballet dancers before them.

The String Band still resonated in my day-to-day existence. They'd produced a few songs about lighthouses in their final years, with another ISB hero, the mighty Malcolm Le Maistre, on vocals. I was now fixated by them and read all I could about life in the middle of the ocean.

One day, still retching from the previous night's medication I espied a job advert in The Sun newspaper, 'Wanted. Lighthouse keeper'.

"That's for me" I thought. "Yes." I'd get a badge and a uniform and show Malcolm! Hoisted to work by helicopter.

Not 'arf!

The wages were not great, but my stoned-self became infatuated at the prospect of getting a 'Rock Allowance' as compensation for a three-month shift staring blankly at the sea, able to tinker with the curtains' open. I believe there's actually a term called a 'Lighthouse Keeper's Wrist'.

A few weeks later I was thrilled to see a letter on the mat with the word 'Lighthouse' on a red stamp at the top. All I could think of was that gold buttoned uniform and showing it off to Malcolm.

'Dear Mr Blacknell,

Thank you for your very interesting letter. Would you like to attend?' Etc. Whoop went my heartstrings. 'Gimme that rock allowance baby!'

It was a rare journey to London – but necessary for the prospective job in hand, so I thought I'd make an effort! The first step was borrowing an oversized toilet brown coloured suit from one of Phil's neighbours – and washing my flowing locks that had bits of Malvern nesting in there. A green and white spotted tie, my trusty blue platform shoes, and my waist length brown hair now tied back.

I looked like a sort of drugged up 'Mr Potato Man'. Nothing fitted – and even I knew I looked very odd indeed. Nevertheless

– as I gazed out of the train window to Worcester to get my connection – the dreams still filled my head, and as I popped my fourth Dodo of the day, it all lay clear before me.

The interview in Pimlico, with a portly bespectacled lighthouse man, was mercifully brief and I was soon back home to contemplate this airy-fairy Quantum Leap into heaven knows what.

It was three weeks later that another red envelope plopped onto the doormat. Tentatively I opened it.

'Dear Mr Blackwell', it began – which was a good start.

'We enjoyed meeting you. Your energy and enthusiasm were duly noted. However, we also note that you list your main hobbies as meeting new people and live music. You also state that you are afraid of deep water. On consideration, we have concluded that perhaps this job is not right for you at this particular time.' A phrase I would hear all too many times in the years to come!

Within a few minutes I was onto new thoughts and greener pastures.

Upon reflection, thank God I didn't get the job as my liver would have fallen out and my right wrist would have fallen off.

As a lad I'd always been able to escape the playground bully by playing the fool. It was indeed my humorous bent that was at the heart of some early conquests with the opposite sex. I was, in truth, not an early starter, preferring a ruck on the rugby field to a roll in the hay.

Sheila, my dusky seducer, seemed light years away – so maybe I was looking for my first romance now, and despite a few excess pounds and my hippy dippy appearance I did manage to get off with the odd 'looker'! I made them laugh. Pure and simple.

Late one Saturday evening at Phil's flat, joss sticks pumping clouds of near toxic fountains of sickly smoke around the room with Beefheart growling gloomily through towering speakers, the doorbell rang.

There, standing in the doorway, was a beautiful lithe damsel - long brown flowing hair – half-way down her back, none on her head – just down her back – (apologies - couldn't resist) and a token yet eye-catching flower power skirt draped around her lower bits to the floor.

"This is Jan," proclaimed Phil, "She's a model, and LOVES the String Band!"

"Pardon meeeee?" I could feel my arm hairs perking in time with my long dormant nether regions.

We clicked like maraca magnets - and within days we were meeting at various pubs and cafes around town, and I was in a right tizz.

Indeed there seemed something there – and I was a very happy lad although I was still trying to shed my prop forward fat.

It was one rainy night at The Malvern Gardens... the gig where the ISB had played a few years before, that we sat drinking wine in the foyer. I was, in truth, quite new at all of this, but we were well on the way to consummating our now blossoming relationship and I was fair frothing at the mouth! "You know what?" she said between sips, "I think you're a lovely guy, but I think you're the fattest man I've ever been out with!

My world crumbled in a second.

I suddenly felt gross, ugly and utterly useless. I felt deflated, disgusted and destroyed. I was crying deep down and just got up and left. Once home I crumbled into a heap, and sobbed my way through till dawn.

That was the last time I saw her. I made excuses about going back to Kent for a break and hid myself in Malvern's finest cubby holes until I felt the 'heat' was off!

It was there – then - that rainy night in that famous ancient spa town that the seeds were sown of an illness that would haunt me and stay with me for far too long.

CHAPTER 9

The First Love

A Bit Later

As always when things went tits up, I'd flee back to the relative sanctity of Dartford and my long-suffering family. The bedroom wall was still there, still layers thick in musical heroes, the wall now added to by newer heroes.

I embarked on a series of very different jobs – as a tea boy on an oil rig, a telephone directory enquiries chap, a postman, pizza delivery boy – the list goes on.

I was on a day off one blustery autumnal rainy day. Bouncing down into Dartford town, I espied the back end of another Steve – a good mate of mine arm in arm with an auburn-haired girl. I shouted his name and as he turned to acknowledge me, so did she. I knew then, maybe, for the first time in my life, I had 'that' feeling.

This was like a bolt from the blue, and somehow, I've never known how – I got her number, and my 'good chum' and her were totally history! Her baby brown eyes entranced me. She felt so familiar to me, as if I'd known her for years.

She was a vegetarian. Strangely my thirst for all things vegetable grew radically over the next few days, and before long we had made a connection. We spoke on the phone a few times - met – and very soon I was head over platform heels in love with one Kate Bush.

I was once more in the clouds. I would play her the ISB… which she loved. Even better.

It soon became apparent that she wrote the odd tune or two and had some connections with the music biz, but I had a big problem. I so wanted to be a part of the business - it hurt me to think that she might make it and I would just be a nobody. In other words, I was jealous as could be and totally up myself, but happy as could be that I was in the company of someone who had such magic surrounding her.

I always told her that the day I got into the 'biz', that would be the day I would listen to her music. So modest was she, so understanding. She had an amazing family around her... who only ever treated me with love and respect.

The two of us would plot and plan world domination; she the pop star and me introducing her on 'Top of the Pops'.

We knew something was in the air.

But I had no real idea that I was dealing with a real top to toe musical genius.

Weirdly, via a contact with the ISB, I landed an interview with Decca Records for a job as a Pop Marketing Assistant for the princely sum of £2,300 a year!

I knew I was ready. A few weeks later a letter plip plopped onto the doormat telling me I had the gig and was to start. Unable to control myself, I called Kate and told her I was at last going to be part of the business that I so yearned for.

That evening she sat me on a sofa in the corner of her family lounge and asked me to turn my back. I duly did. The piano burst into life and two of the most amazing songs I had ever heard sprang into life. One was *'The Saxophone Song'* and the other eludes me but delivered by the voice of an angel. As the last note disappeared, she asked me to turn around. I couldn't really take it in. That was Kate. Once more the power of speech eluded me.

We were so in love it was nuts. I adored so many things about her wonderful self. She was, as now, a very private person and incredibly self-effacing about her music, as well as being wonderfully non-possessive and so proud of my dreams coming true before her eyes.

Aside from the ISB she took a keen interest in the bands I was working with including the very Pinky Floyd'ish yet original 'prog rock band; Camel. We went to see them live and she loved them.

Although the mists of time have clouded various interludes of what is five decades ago, I do recall that things were starting to happen for young Ms Bush. I began to hear of her working with Bowie's former dance teacher, Lindsay Kemp, and a certain David Gilmour. She was a very busy Ms B.

By the end of 1975 things were beginning to hot up for her, and I could sense there may be no place for me anymore. Although it was her decision to part, I, like so many around her, just knew her career was going to happen. She gave me a few acetates, demo '45 rpm discs of Wuthering

Heights, and I gave one to both the late Eddie Pumer who was head of the Capital Radio playlist, and Keith Rogers, an old chum at Ipswich independent station Radio Orwell. Who played what and whether EMI got the first play I don't recall but the fact that her unfeasibly original take on the nineteenth century Bronte tale created shockwaves in the pop world and far beyond, and aside from any personal upset, I recall being thrilled and so, so proud when the world opened its heart to her.

To this very day I still relish those wonderful days when she discovered the delights of all things 'Incredible' and she used to refer to me as '*Red Hair*', a String Band tune she adored so much. I was so very sad saying goodbye to her lovely parents who I'd become so very fond of, and the rest of the Bush ensemble who would contribute so much to those early formative years.

I was and indeed still feel so proud to have known the gentle genius that continues to enthral the planet.

CHAPTER 10

It's Tough in the Middle
1975

I'd met the lovely bubbly Cathy through my time with the ISB. She'd found a lovely flat in Battersea, Worfield Street just a rolling stones' throw away across the Thames from Decca. It was perfect. I revelled in attending our weekly marketing meetings speeding like a twat. I'd down a few 'blues' just before I left the flat, knowing that the full surge of amphetamine-isation would hit me just as proceedings were starting. It enabled me to appear interested in the latest single from Morris bloody Albert or Typically Tropical... or any of the plethora of releases we pumped out. But I relished my chance and I adored having a real job in a real record company.

Since 1929, Decca had been a giant of its times... with everyone from Bing Crosby to Al Jolson to The Stones running through their portals. Of course, they did have the somewhat dubious privilege of signing Brian Poole & The Tremeloes, rather than the Fab Four – but they'd recovered well, and were still held in huge regard by the industry.

I even shared a secretary! The highly desirable Carol Goldsmith or Miss Goodbody, as she was affectionately referred to, who was already an experienced record biz lady. She was a ravishingly petite girl – a few years my senior maybe - but WOW! So, there I was on the floor of the legendary Albert Embankment with an office and a secretary. She took me by the apron strings and showed me how it all worked.

All I had to do was to say yes to my new boss, Alan Fitter, who was very welcoming and took me under his wing. This was my first real job in the pop world – and I just nodded my way through the first year – filling out form after form. Across the corridor were the A&R team fronted by the legendary pipe smoker and top toff, Hugh Mendel.

He had a lovely man working with him called Frank Rodgers, brother to the late Clodagh, no less, who'd go on to marry Ms Goldsmith and sign Thin Lizzy, gasp, and there was another nice bloke called Nick Tauber who was more a producer, I think, but it was a merry team.

My job was to write out the Decca releases and comment on them for the sales force – so they had some clue as to what wares they were flogging. I was a pig in shit. Easy peeeezy! We had parties every month and all sorts of stars would turn up for a glass of lukewarm Blue Nun in a wafer-thin plastic cup and a warmed-up Co-Op sausage roll. But it did put the rock into the roll!'

Mr Fitter was a good man and we started to gel on music trivia and the like. So much so that he asked me to co-compile a Procol Harum 'Roots' compilation, which thrilled me to bits. I had no idea what the hell I was doing but having loved the band for so long, it was not that hard. I was also hauled in to help compile the Stones' 'Rolled Gold' double album which again tickled my fickle fancy.

With my suave devil-may-care looks and long flowing locks, I now looked the part. So much so that Fitter explained that Graeme Edge, from the Moodies, had a solo album called *'Kick Off your Muddy Boots'* coming out. Despite Graeme having a band, it was actually Adrian and Paul Gurvitz who provided most of the action... and they wanted a trendy rocker on the cover!

I was ferried over to a huge West London mansion for a photoshoot! I arrived in Levi jeans and shirt, freshly hennaed hair and a beating heart! I'd been shitting for England that morning and I was hoping I wasn't going to do a whoopsee on his very expensive sofa.

The results were pretty good. My nose seemed twenty sizes bigger on the shot, but who was I to comment.

My nose had always run in the family.

Could this be it? I could see it now - my moosh in Woolworths staring back at me from the record rack. Yesssss.

A few weeks later Alan called me in to his office and informed me that, although I'd done really well, they had decided to go with another idea. The gig had gone to some artist bloke called Roger Dean, who went on to do rather well.

Aside from my beloved Camel and John Miles, Caravan were my Decca fave rave band, they were and still are my all-time trippy hippy outfit. I'd LSD'd my arse off five years earlier to classics like *'In the Land of the Grey and Pink'* off the proverbial trolley.

So, when the boss asked me if I'd like to come up with a very punny title for their next album, their latest 'prog-pop' platter, I was thrilled. The band had always liked using puns as titles and I had the revelatory idea of a cover photo of an ageing mucky tree with a dog poo at the base.

'Dirty Tree and A Turd', a pun on the 33/3rd speed of LPs came to me whilst in an eatery in Kings Road one morning at 1am. I was sure this would hit the spot.

It didn't.

'Cunning Stunts' came out that July to critical acclaim. So near yet so fucking far. The signs were being writ in them stars, as in so near yet so faaaaar away!

The Moody Blues were signed to Decca through their own label, Threshold, and I'd often see Justin Hayward or John Lodge floating in and out. 'It's them', I'd mutter to myself. The bands *'Threshold of a Dream'* had been a huge 'tripping' album in Cornwall. I could NOT believe I was but a few feet away from them!

Later on, my involvement with Denny *'Go Now'* Laine would become a bit more personal. Little did I know!

CHAPTER 11

Meeting Maggie

1976

In truth, everything must be for a reason. There are NO coincidences, no way! Already my life appeared to be laden with odd events and strange connections. By then, I was happily ensconced within the 'very straight' Decca marketing department at Albert Embankment.

I'd seen jazz/prog/rock combo Steamhammer at the Plumpton Festival and blow me down I was now their former vocalists record plugger.

So, I was asked by my boss to go and visit vocalist Kieran White in North London to collect some of his first efforts since signing his deal. I rang the doorbell of his ground floor flat, nerves a-jangling.

A thin balding man in rocker T-shirt and jeans opened the door.

"Hi mate, I'm Steve from... Decc ..."

I stopped dead in my tracks as a pair of familiar eyes poked over his right shoulder through the hallway haze.

Oh, mother of pearl! I knew those eyes. They were brown as bark and bright as the sun, and for a milli-second I was back in Dartford.

Our eyes were fixed together, "This is Maggie," he muttered.

Later at home I just couldn't get them out of my head. The same look. That auburn hair and those tawny eyes!

It would take some four and a half decades in the future for that to surface once more.

Maggie had originally worked at Island Records looking after the genial Brian Eno but she was now at WEA Records, that's all I knew, or that's all he'd told me, and, once again, I was thrown completely off my stride. A wonder of a woman, but with someone else!

As before, I can't remember how I got her number, but I did, and just like before, this other man was instant history!

I called her. In a somewhat bizarre billing, John Miles was supporting ex-Procol Harum turned guitar God, Robin Trower, at the Manchester Free Trade Hall. Might she like to come? John would be previewing his new single, *'Music',* and again I had that funny feeling that I was involved in something very special.

The gig, on a cold wet February day was like no other I'd ever seen. I was shaking with pride that little old me actually knew that man on stage, it was totally unreal! So too was the brown eyed beauty next to me.

I could feel the electricity between us bouncing back and forth like passion popping ping pong balls. She had beguiling eyes and that wild brunette vibe I so loved. It felt so empowering. Was it love? Lust? Very soon we both knew it was indeed something special.

The train journey back to London was over in a flash and a flurry that denied nature. We were glued together, oblivious to the outside world. We were the only people alive. I'm certain we tried to achieve the 4-foot-6-inch-high club, but the mists have never really cleared from that extraordinary day.

"Well, invite me in, you silly bugger," she said, now tugging me into my Battersea doorway. I was never blokeish, and it was clear the next move had to come from her.

It was a night like no other, and as the first light of dawn melted through the flimsy curtains, for me at least, the axis of the Earth had tilted.

Might it even last? Could this *Brown Eyed Girl* be THE one so soon after Kate and I had parted company? It was a long night of unbridled passion... the best two minutes of her bloody life I can tell you, and once more I was totally, blissfully in love. We became as solid as the proverbial rock.

I was now making in-roads at my Decca job – which was handily just a pebbles' throw from my flat.

Maggie had now joined a new promotions company in their Wardour Street office – looking after former Ten Years After guitar whizzkid, Alvin Lee, and the infamous *'Baker Street'* luminary, Gerry Rafferty.

Maggie was Halifax born and bred and didn't mince her words. When I played her 'Wuthering Heights' she was sufficiently blown away to put it in front of her boss's beady eyes. "Rubbish!" had been his terse response. We'd play it often but I'd try to keep the Bush Telegraph machine to a minimum as it had only been a few months since we'd split and I didn't want to rock and roll the brand-new love boat!

A few months in, we were as tight as a duck's botty and were living the dream, yet there were a few things she had to get out of her system and left me for a month to visit her favourite Greek island – Santorini.

Meanwhile back at the ranch, on the other side of the Thames in downtown Soho sat the infamous Decca promotions department, nicknamed 'The Fairy Grotto', appertaining to the fact that every boss in living memory had not only 'batted for the other side' but had made the tea and sandwiches too.

Being the mid-seventies, it raised no more than a mild titter and indeed it was no great shakes. The shining star and totally straight, (well he was when I slept with him) was a dynamo of a man called Jeremy Thomas. 'Lord' Thomas's reputation went miles before him. Bubbling with energy, loved by all and genial with the artists, his shaggy, tousled black hair and ill-fitting suits marked him out from the crowd. When I spotted him in the office opposite, I often wondered what it might be like to be him?

He was a bit of genius it has to be said, and it was no surprise at our weekly meet that we were all informed that Lord T was leaving Decca to form his very own label, Electric Records. Despite my very public relationship with Kate, with my girly looks, long brown hair and eyes of bloodshot with a mild hint of blue, it was the general consensus that I too enjoyed a man snog.

But that call from Jeremy changed my life.

"Lord Blacknell," he pronounced loudly in a call one day. "I'm suggesting you for my job as a Radio One plugger… I know you can do it." I was bowled over like a tenpin spare. "Thanks JT," I spat disbelievingly into the phone. "I won't let you down."

As it happens I didn't. Jeremy took with him the wondrous and legendary 'Five Star Annie Piper' - a brunette beauty who went on to marry the wonderful and sadly missed, Big Three/Roxy Music legend, Johnny Gustafson, who left us years ago.

My relatively painless entry into the glittering world of music 'promo' was complete.

Maggie was to be a wonderful constant in my life. Quiet - yet with a sparkling energy that enthralled - and beautifully blunt with it.

It was a combination many men found irresistible – including yours truly. In truth she could have had the pick of the male species but always went for those who made her laugh. Thank the Lord I have a funny streak – otherwise, no chance mate.

She also had her spell of rock & roll romances – including the very man wot did the foreword – the geezer 'imself, Mr Bill Wyman esq. and a lovely bonding with the late Tom Petty. Check out the track '*Magnolia*', on the album '*You're gonna Get It!*' which was from him to her.

Bless him.

CHAPTER 12

Here Comes Mr PR!

Sometime in the Seventies

Now this podgy ex-hippy was thrown into a whole new world, full of razzle dazzle, and like the duck to water, I revelled in the sheer pomp and ridiculousness of it all. Drink by the bucketful and constant entertaining in the finest restaurants saw the pounds pile on.

Lo and behold the very first record I was told to take to the Radio One 'palace of pain' was by a brand-new star. The Decca PR machine was now trying to morph their exciting new signing, John Miles, into a 70s James Dean, but it didn't seem to be working

At just under six minutes long, '*Music'* felt far too long to stand a chance at Radios 1 and 2, but we could give it a go! Thankfully for John, I was still learning from the established team, and although it was they, not I, who eventually got John to number one and global glory, I was chuffed to be involved and dined out on it whenever humanly possible. Dear, dear John – one of the loveliest and most talented people I ever met. He could have been another Elton John... but the fickle finger of fate would deny the world his true genius.

He is missed by so many.

I was not only 'plugging' Decca stuff but their other labels too, so one minute I'd be working on a Threshold Moody Blues project, the next on another offering from a sister label.

Most of these labels would have an unlikely hit then build the label around that. Indeed, Gull was no different, and despite their lack of success with Mr White's Steamhammer, had scored an unlikely summer hit in '75 with Typically Tropical's one-off chart topper, '*Barbados.'* Amongst their other acts were budding superstars, Judas Priest, which meant extended visits Brumward's to hang out with Rob Halford and company. Also, I had amazing times with a lovely folkie, Steve Ashley, late of the Ashley Hutchins band, who I STILL dote on, and the UK jazzers, If, along with an utterly brilliant German jazz rock band called Kraan. I'd seen them in concert in town and was determined to get them on the legendary TV rock show, The Old Grey Whistle Test.

What that meant was to go and inhabit the show's office opposite BBC TV Centre at every weak opportunity and fire the band's name into the producers' faces until they maybe came to a gig to see if they were suitable. The daddy of Rock TV, the icon that was the now sadly departed Michael Appelton, was 'God' and if you could get to him, you might stand a chance. The OGWT could make or break a band. It must be said, though, that the show itself was a 'pick and mix' affair and if the line-up needed a jazz or blues act and you happened to be in the right time and place with a talent they needed, then happy days!

It was a steamy summer's day in downtown Newcastle, and I was just waking up in the hotel after 'plugging' my bloody brains out to the local radio station when the phone burst to life... "Hello, Steve? This is Michael here." Michael? I shrugged.

"Yes, Michael Appleton - your boys - Kraan, are on next week's show."

JOY! Sheer, unabashed, unremitting, pant-shitting joy! "Oh, thanks Mike, erm, that's... er... wow..." Click.

That feeling - was soooo major...

I'd done it! 'Shit me - this is easy.' I thought later – piece of piss!

Erm, well no, it wasn't, isn't or never will be. I got lucky. You gotta have luck!

Be ready too, and when your chance flows by, jump in big time!

The Radio One DJs were like gods back then. Dave Lee Travis, Tony Blackburn, Noel Edmunds, and of course Alan 'Fluff' Freeman, best known for presenting the stations' 'Pick of the Pops' from 1961 to 2000, sadly passing away six years later. The Oz born entertainer had been a fixture on the UK media scene with his smarmy TV ads to become a national treasure in radio land.

This pre-Saville media world was delightfully awash with all kinds of gay everything, as noted - I myself was prescribed homosexual before I could open my gob. But it was all very free and there seemed, somehow, less pressure than today over who does what, with who.

CHAPTER 13

A Tap on the Shoulder

1976 (it was a busy year)

Since my 'Whistle Test' success I was, as they say, on a roll, and I soon found myself out at a business lunch with Mr Appleton himself, along with a few BBC types, and Alan 'Fluff' Freeman himself. I was overawed, lost for words. The venue was a tippy toppy posh eatery in London's trendy Holland Park.

A place that would become very important to me seven years later.

One of the main points of the event was to plug '*Moon Madness',* the new album by label stalwarts, Camel.

It had been nigh on a decade since I'd been called 'fat' by the Malvern lass who'd sent me into a tizzy. I'd noticed of late that my normally trim figure was filling out somewhat! Those tell-tale signs - the dreaded belt loop syndrome and tight-fitting jackets.

Suddenly I'd been transported to another world. A far cry from fire extinguishers and mid-sea ocean gazing. This was the rock & roll life I'd always dreamt of. But I needed to fit in to the thin way of life and quick! But how?

So it was on that day that something deep inside snapped like a mouse-trap.

An incredibly strange feeling of total emptiness. It bounced around my body like a rancid rubber ball. Amongst all this excitement, a spring had sprung.

As the drinks were poured and poured, so I felt emptier and emptier. I needed filling up... input - mass. What a fucking weird feeling.

I couldn't grasp it. What WAS happening to me?

Out came the menus. Lots of strange foreign things I'd never heard of. But as I furiously drank white wine glass after glass, nodding to my esteemed company, I found myself ordering a king prawn cocktail.

At least I knew what that was!

Not normally a gulper of food, I found myself shovelling it down like cement into a dirty ditch. It didn't touch the sides, gone - in three swallows. Then followed breadsticks and huge bread rolls with butter… mountains of butter. Full, I felt really full, with a weird mix of delight and displeasure. It's often said that addicted gamblers sometimes get lost in the moment and 'come to' entrenched in a casino or a losing card game, likewise, alcoholics blink and find themselves gripping a glass.

Then – it came.

It was as if an imaginary force was tapping me on the shoulder.

I suppose I must have excused myself from the table, but all I can recall is finding myself in the very posh toilet! Staring at my bulging tummy, I panicked and before I knew it my second and third fingers of my right hand were halfway down my throat - probing - then pushing for all they were worth - then I felt it. Like a volcano, deep down slowly starting to erupt. Then, it all came – up into my over-stretched open mouth and whoosh into the toilet bowl. A putrid pink acidic mush. A waterfall of waste now belched below, and then - silence.

I found myself peering downwards - eager to inspect. So, there it all was, and with a swipe of the flush, it wasn't. It had gone.

Staring into the mirror with blinking eyes, I could feel a rush and a tingle climbing through my body into my brain. I lifted my shirt and the bulge had gone. Mr Tummy was flat not fat. Oh, the joy. Oh, the sheer flushing joy of it all!

Elated, I rejoined the throng, drinking several more wines before the overlarge steak main course dutifully plopped before my now hungry eyes. Once more I slung it down in record time. Once more I excused myself from the proceedings and, once more the finger brothers did their work and very soon a rib of beef, three roast potatoes and some delicately peppered buttered broccoli, were on their way to Brighton. The same fate would befall a hunk of brandied chocolate cheesecake and a whirl of whipped cream. I sat there beaming. I was shaking, I felt amazing. This was fucking incredible - I could eat and be thin, YESSS. With the downing of a few large brandies, I started to buzz.

This was pure magic and indeed the icing on the erm - cake! This was also the start of what would become a terrible wasting disease that would change my way of life and put my very being in harm's way.

With the lunch now over, and ALL of mine having successfully arrived at the seaside, I said a fond farewell to the lovely Fluff. What a LOVELY man!!!

The following Monday morning I was summoned to my boss's office.

"Alan would love you to go round to his house in Maida Vale and take the Camel album so he can hear it," came the order. "Okay great," I said, excited at the prospect of seeing Alan in his own space. Just him and little old meeee!!!

"Do come in love," Fluff waved me in. "Whisky?"

"Erm - great, yes thanks." I stuttered as I backed into the humongous, patterned sofa. In the shake of a tail, Alan was plunked next to me, aftershave wafting out from beneath his dressing gown.

"Cheers!"

Even for a twenty-five-year-old, I was a bit thin under the cap and it was only as I felt his hand on my knee that it occurred to me what was up.

"I'm not gay you know, Alan," I whispered quietly. The response was swift and sure.

"Oh, sorry my love, I've been misinformed," came the retort.

I left a few awkward minutes later, and I left the album too.

Alan's Radio One 'Saturday Rock show' was always a high point of my week, and I'd always stretch out on my favourite patch of Battersea Park on a Saturday afternoon and listen intently. As I lay musing over the previous day's misunderstanding, I chuckled at how gracious he was amid the confusion. Was that the way the music business *really* worked. I couldn't work it out.

But then, the strains I knew so well, that lunar sound, came echoing over the airwaves from my small transistor. Side one of *'Moon Madness'*. Dearest Fluff was playing it. And play it he did... the entire first side!

Even in those wide-eyed, leggy days of the music biz it appeared there was still honour amongst the weird and wacky world of Rock and Roll!

CHAPTER 14

Anything for a Plug or Two & 'Doing A Carnaby'

1976

By now, Maggie and I were as one as two could ever be – and set out to find the appropriate love nest to settle down in and pat our feathers dry. Holland Road was, and still is, a pretty high falutin proper posh area of West London. The nearby Holland Park was choc-a-bleedin-block with mansions and the like – terminally trendy and a ballbreaking fortune to live there. As I would find out a little later on.

It was Holland Road we settled on, a lovely ground floor affair, loads of space and a garden so small you couldn't swing a baby rat in it!

I said a sad bye-bye to Cathy and co and we moved in lock, stock and a barrel or three to our new super trendy love shack.

Upstairs were a wild and woolly couple; Johnny, a stout late fifties figure of a man - resplendent in a military jacket straight out of Rorke's Drift, and his mental Peruvian Mrs. We were immediately submerged in their crazy circle of screwed up nutty pals. Huge amounts of home-made wine were consumed and we very often fell down the stairs in a vain attempt to reach the flat before we were sick everywhere.

Maggie had joined 'me old mate' Bob Harris at the new company 'Wilde Rock Promotions' and we'd often go to dinner at his West London gaff. He was, as he is now, a delightful and easy going chap and I recall one Saturday night affair where he put a portable TV on the dinner table to watch 'Match of the Day', much to the amusement of the assembled dinner guests.

I'd joined the Anchor Records team in Wardour St. - They were the English arm of ABC in the USA, so I was now promoting the likes of Steely Dan, Ace, Poco and two of the biggest Country and Western stars on the planet; Don Williams, and the wonder that was the legendary George Hamilton the Fourth.

I had two team mates; Tim, the loud, feisty bespectacled trend bomb, and Dave, who had bought a very different leather clad 25-year-old girly from Akron, Ohio to our attention, and who would go on to be at the core of the career of one Chrissie Hynde. Then there was me, still very wet behind the earlobes, but the office nice guy! It was a wonderful time, where money would never be a problem.

Amongst my duties was to visit Downtown Radio in Newtownards, County Down, Northern Ireland. I had made great friends out there including the playlist lady - one of nature's gems, Gina, I think it was. She was the PR people's favourite with her easy-going ways and a likeability factor that was off the scale.

"Sue, can you book me a three day return to Belfast?" I yelled across the hubbub of the crowded office. So, via the customary cab to Heathrow, I was soon touching down on the tarmac of Belfast. There, as always, would be a few of the station 'jocks' - the wisecracking Hendi Henderson or the irrepressible Big T – who always said he put the C*** into Country and Western.

They would always be there to greet me – both clutching a bottle of Bush - Bushmills whisky and a bottle of 'white' lemonade. Then it would begin. For three days, no sleep, party time, and enough booze to sink Stormont.

The mid-seventies were a time of 'the troubles' and it was indeed a very precarious place to be.

My great DJ pal, Eddie West, and I were visiting a pub on a hill just outside of Newtownards one sunny Saturday, and as I strode up to the bar I had only just uttered, "Hello mate," to the barman when I felt a huge hand on my shoulder, Eddie whispering loudly, "Feckin' shut it, Stevie, let me do the ordering!!" Indeed, it didn't pay to openly advertise ones London roots back then and, as I sat gingerly in the corner, so Eddie procured drinks in his familiar brogue.

Two hours later, after several pints and chatting about everything except my products, Eddie turned to me. "One for the frog 'n toad Stevie?"

"Nah," I said, "Let's make for the radio station, eh?"

As the pub became smaller in the distance, an enormous BOOM shook the vehicle and we could see in the car mirrors a huge plume of smoke engulf all around. It was only later we heard that a bomb had exploded in the very same pub we had just left. We were almost caught up in it! From that day on, I never ever ordered a drink in Belfast.

Indeed, it pays to go with the 'when in Rome' theory.

I realized I was a mere beginner, with a long messy path ahead. It was one of my real experiences of sheer unadulterated excess. And I LOVED it!

Indeed, there was once where I found myself in a hotel bed next morning with the DJ I'd been out to dinner with, totally pissed and passed out.

One time I hit the office straight from Heathrow. "How was the trip, Steve?" yelled Sue. "Any luck with Steely Dan?" Oh, FUCKKKKKK rang my brain alarm, the whole point of these trips was to sweeten the DJ with meals and drinks then go for the jugular. Anything to get your record played on the station.

In my excitement to get over there, I'd totally forgotten to pack my records. In fact, I hadn't even discussed music at all! "With you in a mo," I yelled back, and, in a heartbeat, I was talking on the phone to the playlist lady I'd been getting trashed with the night before. "It goes like this", I started to whistle the *'Haitian Divorce'* tune down the phone. "Okay, Stevie - love it - it's on the playlist," came the retort. "

"Sue!" I shouted, "I've got it on the A list."

"Yay!" everyone yelled. "BLACK-NELL... BLACK-NELL!"

Flipping nuts – totally ridiculous.

I was now looking after the careers of the wondrous Cado Belle – a Scottish funk band fronted by the lovely Maggie Reilly, who'd later go on to global fame as the ridiculously unaccredited voice of the Mike Oldfield hit *'Moon Shadow'*. I had a blast touring the UK and beyond, and, as if by fate, following on from Mr Miles' *'Music'* an epic five-minute opus, Steely Dan's *'Haitian Divorce'* slightly longer in length confirmed my credentials as a plugger with promise. In those innocent times, London's very own Capital Radio would have a peoples vote thingy to get songs into their chart.

It was indeed farcical as the entire staff would be constantly calling in with a bizarre range of voices.

White/black/yellow/gruff/ high-pitched, you name it, it was ridiculous, but it worked! The Dan became a hit despite its unlikely length, so jobby done!

My burgeoning Bulimia had started to screw my system up, and my bowels were irregular to say the least! I hadn't been to 'biggies' for four days. It was 8.45am on a cold grey winter's morn and I exited the tube at Piccadilly Circus bound for the London HQ. As the bitter wind hit home on my bones, I felt a strange sensation down below where one's colon connects to one's arse.

As I hurried down Carnaby Street, a sharp pain hit my gut and slowly the true horror of the situation hit me. I was going to park my breakfast.

As my pace quickened, so the sweat began to roll down both types of cheeks, and in one horrifying moment I realised I had given birth to nearly four days blockage. I stood motionless. What now I thought? Although the stores were still shut, I could see a figure in a menswear establishment moving about in the doorway. It was, in fact, an Indian cleaner lady. So, I waddled up to her penguin like. "I'm sorry," I said, "But I've had an accident can you help?" She showed me to the staff toilet and I slid my credit card under the door. "Please get me some trousers?" I said, as you do. It was a very messy interlude, which saw me emerge thirty minutes later in a pair of ill-fitting shorts and several unpleasant smelling carrier bags.

Once at the office, I made excuses and ordered a cab. Layering several copies of Music Week on the seat of the taxi, I perched precariously during the 40-minute journey home.

Still white as a sheet, and trembling with the after effects – now cleansed - I called Maggie who was in a work meeting. "Sweetie – please don't mention to anyone, but I've just shit my pants in Carnaby Street." There was silence until I heard her shriek "Guess what? STEVE JUST SHIT HIS PANTS in Carnaby Street!"

It was just two weeks later that I'd turned up for the staff morning meeting after being up all-night drinking with some chums. Some ten minutes into the proceedings, I noticed a few of the attendees sniffing and grimacing, so much so that I joined in. "What a stink!" Then one of the secretaries pointed at my shirt sleeve. "Oh JEEZUZ!" she yelled. I looked down and sure enough my left sleeve had the remains of a vegetable Dansak smeared all over. I then remembered we had ordered in a curry very late on... and I had brought at least half of it to work. Still... marvellous silly times.

But it was going to get VERY silly indeed!

CHAPTER 15

Stan An-De-liver

I'm Certain it's 1976

I'll never forget walking into a very basic bar just outside Newcastle with John Miles and one of his band whereupon, after rather gingerly asking for a bottle of Pils lager, the burly barman yelled loudly... "What are yer? A poof like man? I'll give yer two bottles and put 'em in a fooking pint glass!"

That was me told.

Still, I've always loved that Northern spirit, and through those promo years we'd spend more and more time 'up Norf' with my musical chums like John, infamous folk guitarist Michael Chapman, and Cado Belle. The trick I was once told was "Just don't be a dick or try to be clever and you'll be alright." Something which I never forgot.

The best quote of all came from a coal miner called Stan, a customer in a little watering hole in Cumbria I'd frequent with my folkie pals, Chapman, Steeleye etc. Stan was well known for his ability to consume insane amounts of booze. After a day down the local mine... still sooty, with big panda eyes and complete with flat cap... he'd merrily sup 14 pints a night, hastily followed by countless Pernod and Grapefruits. Even at the tender age of twenty-four, I thought I could tuck a few away, but Stan was in a different chuffing league - I was intrigued. "Stan... how the hell do you do that?" I enquired. "Well, Mr Blacknell," he bellowed, "Tis easy man... I've had me stomach taken oot and a bucket poot in!" I was in awe, real men, nuffink like down Souf!

CHAPTER 16

What A Dope!

1976... I think

Meanwhile back on the lurve train, Maggie and I were now like two lovesick bugs in a very large rug, and there was no stopping us in every respect of the word.

The local Italian eatery and pissery, Franco Ovest, in Russell Gardens, just by the BBC, would be the chosen destination on a Friday lunchtime, following after the *Breakfast Time* 9am piss up in Shepherd's Bush at Albertines, which was the wine bar in question as soon as the cameras ceased to roll, the entire presentation staff would leg it down there for an early drink.

As the BBC *Breakfast Time's* pop presenter, I had my very own producer, Daf Daly, was her name. A lovely funny Brum lady who would magic pop stars out of their beds to come and face me live on telly.

Maggie and I loved Franco's too. We'd have a bucket of wine in the flat, order a taxi on expenses to pick us up and drive us the four hundred yards there, then crawl up the five steps and plop down at our favourite table by the window. Suitably oiled, some three hours later, we'd order another cab to ferry what was left of us the four hundred yards back home. Wonderful fun!

Franco the boss was an ebullient fat chap who grinned and shouted smut at the girls all the time. We loved him. Rather unfortunately, he was nicked by the police when someone discovered a peep hole and a camera in one of the walls of the ladies' loo, and we never went back after that. But wonderful times.

It was a rainy night in High St Kensington and I'd grabbed some tickets for a media movie night.

And so, togged up to the nines, we cabbed there and were walking across the reception floor when Maggie tugged at my coat. "Jeezuz, look who it is." There – stepping down the huge stairs - arm in arm with a dark-haired man was the shapely shape of Miss Kate Bush herself.

"Look" I cried. "She's wearing make-up!"

She'd never been one for the theatrical slap, and it was quite a shock.

We exchanged smiles across the reception floor and Maggie told me later their eyes met in one single moment she'd never forget.

So, a tingle crept up my spine and my arm hairs rose to attention. It was a lovely moment, and I can recall thinking 'Go on Kate – you do it, girl'. By March 1978 she had. And although I'd had to make way for her career, I was as proud as proud could be.

Maggie and I were living in bliss, and all was well. We loved every minute of each other and life was one big adventure.

Until, and I'll never ever know exactly why I did it, whilst on a promotional visit 'up norf' I stupidly slept with the receptionist from Bradford's Pennine Radio. I told Maggie what I had done. It totally screwed us up. I remember thinking, 'There must be other fish in the sea.' But little did I know, there weren't, and I'd just sacrificed the biggest catch of my life!

We parted badly. Not surprising really, but I'll never forget that she still wanted to be friends. That, I did not deserve, and it signalled the start of my inability to hold down a relationship.

We dismantled the love-nest, she moved to North London and I moved over to a house in South Ealing, West London with my good BBC Radio London pal Andy Finney and a few weirdly straight accountants with not a sausage in sight, and there was Mike D, a very strange man who always ate his breakfast from a dog bowl on the kitchen floor. To this day I've never quite fathomed why. I mean, I'd get up to a few nutty things, but that was just plain bonkers weird.

By early '77 I'd been poached to join the plugging ranks of the mighty Chrysalis Records, home to the likes of Leo Sayer, Jethro Tull and my all-time fave live band, New Zealand's outrageous psycho circus combo, Split Enz.

Amongst the other bands I was enthusing about were The Frankie Miller Band. The rough 'n tough Glaswegian's raspy rock vocals had eventually seen both public and critical acclaim with his stunning '*Full House*' album – and they joined an impressive line-up including Thin Lizzy and Aerosmith, watched at an impossibly muddy Reading Festival in 1977.

In truth, by the time they came on that final Sunday, many of the long-suffering audience had legged it due to the atrocious conditions, but they were brilliant and I was dutifully there to support not only them but Chrysalis stable mates, Racing Cars, who'd just enjoyed a huge hit with *'They Shoot Horses Don't They',* and I loved them too.

A few of us were told by those 'up top' to wear the now legendary sweatshirt – with *'Frankie Who?'* on the front top pocket and *'Frankie Fucking Miller That's Who'* emblazoned on the back! We all thought this was a bit of a hoot... and beer bottle in hand I pranced up and down in the gooey mud, loving the shock value!

I felt a sharp tap on my shoulder and there stood Dixon of Shlock Green himself; a stern six-foot helmeted purveyor of the law. "Alright son, you're nicked," he spouted through his chin strap. And before I knew anything, I was bundled into a black van and taken to Reading Police Station - under arrest for obscenity having put a few straight noses out of joint.

I was later released when a Chrysalis suit arrived and did his official bit. An hour later, I was back in the festival mud and not with m'lud. I kept the shirt though, I just wish it fitted now. Isn't it funny that the older you get your clothes start to shrink?

I used to visit Plymouth Sound Radio when the 10pm – midnight DJ at the time was on-air. He was a lovely bloke: a pipe smoking sixty-something smoothie who eased the West Country into the late-night hours, mind you it didn't take much as most of the easy-going populace were half asleep anyway.

Back then when vinyl was king, 'jocks' would often drop the needle down on a track at the beginning, middle and end to save having to listen to the whole thing... thereby getting a feel of the song etc.

I was in the foyer when I saw him emerge from the console. "I need a crap - so I've put a Monty Python album on, and I've listened to a few bits, and it sounds okay. "That'll give me nearly half an hour."

Very soon the strains of Cleese and Co. bounced around the building, as a very different kind of strain echoed from the bog. He told me later that he'd just dropped his trousers as the aforesaid spindly comic was heard to say something along the lines of 'We'd like to warn you of the swearing on this long player... so, there'll be ten fucks, three cunts, an arsehole and five bollocks!"

He literally crapped himself as the barrage of filth hit the Devon airwaves. Helplessly, he sat there convinced his career was at an end.

Not one complaint reached the stations bosses. Makes you wonder doesn't it.

I LOVED getting really stoned as I drove around the South – from Ipswich and Reading to Swansea, and from Portsmouth to Plymouth. I'd eat a big lump of dope-cake in the kitchen then glide gracefully along the many motorways that traversed the area with not a care in the wide-world.

On one particular day, I was halfway to Swansea on the M something or other... well 'off it' and enjoying all the buttons and dials in front of me, windows down, barely touching thirty-five miles an hour, but all was fine with the world. Lorries were passing me, clearly naffed off at the crawler in their way. One hooted.

I was creeping, snail like, now paranoid about my speed in the middle lane when I became aware of a blue flashing light in my mirror.

"Bollocks," I thought. "If they stop me with all this dope I'm carrying, I've had it." Maybe that lorry man had reported me. Panicking in slow mo, I clicked my left indicator and as I drew into the slow lane threw my remaining stash out of the window onto the verge. At least I'll be clean, I thought. My heart missed a beat or three as I observed the blue light whizz past me at a rate of knots and disappear into the distance.

What had I done? Eighty-quid's worth of fine Lebanese gear - GONE! What a twat! I began to panic once more. What should I do? I could make out a sign saying the next exit was three miles away, and it seemed perfectly natural what to do next. As I wibble-wobbled down the turn off, all I could see in my mind's eye was that silver foiled package of joy just waiting for me to bring it home to Daddy.

Some thirty minutes later I'd managed to drop back a few miles and rejoin the road once more. "Now where's that little bugger?" I mouthed to myself. As I wobbled once more, I kept staring at the passing verge, convinced I'd find it. It all seemed very reasonable. I'd find it eventually. Yeah – right!

It must have been a good hour and many miles later that I was still staring glassily through the window as I proceeded ever slower, in case I missed it. Of course, I was nowhere near wherever it had hit the grass and it eventually dawned on me that all was lost.

By the time I'd hit my Swansea hotel, I was ruefully resigned to plan B - alcohol. 'Never mind,' I mused – slugging back a double treble tequila, 'maybe some lucky bunny rabbit might have the night of their life'. However, by now I was as removed as a lucky bunny could be.

I was, by then, not only a full-time bulimic but had added the joys of anorexia to my list of woes. Things had been getting a bit nuts! When I wasn't getting bonked rigid, my everyday was all about shedding the pounds, and I was going to ridiculous ends in my attempts to get thin.

I'd taken to weighing myself at base and shoving the scales in the boot before setting off. I'd then knock back about three or four cans of Diet Coke on the journey, and upon arrival at my desired destination in the hotel or radio station car park, get them out and weigh myself once more. I can only tell of my abject horror if I saw that I hadn't lost any weight in those few hours. It never occurred to me that I had all that liquid in my tum-tum, it just didn't compute. It usually ended up with a scoff and purge episode as I just could NOT figure it out.

In truth, sad times, and it would only get worse.

Of course, the time-honoured art of the fiddling of expenses was as rife as ever. And much as before – we all had agreements with the DJs we 'serviced' the records to. I looked after the south of England and the effervescent energy of Plymouth's 'jocks' who we'd regularly wine and dine in search of that elusive 'Record of the Week'. I'd always get a few blank receipts from the eatery which I'd then claim back as 'lunch with so and so - Plymouth Sound Radio' etc. In fact, I'd make more money on fake receipts than I earned from the company. Bloody luvverly jubbly!!

One Monday morning I got a call from my big boss's secretary asking me to come in immediately! Back then us regional pluggers had the added luxury of working from home – and just banging around our given stations in the company car.

In fact, I'd sometimes lay stoned as shit in my bed – calling my five stations and again whistling the tracks I was meant to be playing them, getting better results and earning great money from fictional receipts. In later years my then boss, a lovely man called Chris Griffin, confessed he knew something was up but couldn't quite put his finger on it. Suffice to say when his wife would let him know my improbable expenses had dropped onto the mat, he'd always grimace as he opened them. Of course, I was not alone in this tomfoolery as most of the music biz was doing it... so it was just a case of getting away with it for as long as one could.

"Now then Steve," grunted Mr Bossman, "I'll come straight to the point. I'm going to have to let you go!" Puzzled, nay fucking bemused, I asked, "Why?"

"Well," he continued, awkwardly clearing his bearded throat, "It appears from your expenses last week – you claimed you'd been with that DJ the week before – but the trouble is that *I* claimed for that too, so one of us is going and it's not gonna be me."

So, for the first and only time in my professional life, I'd been sacked.

'Screw him!' I thought. NEXT!!

Just a few weeks before, I'd been leading Mr Leo Sayers' entourage to a 'live' appearance at Southern TV in Southampton and got lost – losing him the slot. So, I wasn't in the good books anyway. I'd also fallen head over plimsolls in obsession with a 'Kate Bush/Maggie-esque' brown-eyed beauty on a South of England TV station, and I was, of course, besotted. I sent her flowers at alarmingly regular intervals, longing to meet her in person. Once more I'd fallen for those sparklingly bright brown eyes, and, once more, I was helpless.

After several tortuous months, I realised that my quest for the dark eyed beauty was doomed to failure as she had met another and I was history.

CHAPTER 17

Waiter Minute… It's The Booze Brothers

19… not a clue!

I had long been infatuated with the John Landis OTT romp, '*The Blues Brothers.*' So much so that I had started to dress the part around town. Pork pie hat, black tie, white shirt, suit and sunglasses. Don't forget the bleeding sunglasses – vitally important! It soon became an obsession I started to share with Kof, along with two beautiful 'Boozettes' and 'The Booze Brothers' were born. For two years, we would embark on a series of crazed adventures that in terms of 'devil may care' would give the movie a run for its money. No scripts, but a lot of amphetamine sulphate in yoghurt and several visits to Butlins holiday camps where we would stay for days in uniform buggering about and getting up to not much really. But it was all a hoot and innocent fun.

Kof and I had also formed an equally bizarre partnership known as 'Dial a Waiter' where we would serve drinks for business parties in a 'dominantly servile' manner and get completely arsed with our super posh clients. This was Withnail and I on acid - in tuxes. Sheer heaven.

The ruse was to confide in the client ahead of the gig and find out any disturbing or embarrassing facts about their guests that were only known within their circle; perhaps one of them had recently been caught cheating on his wife, or another may have had a drink problem. These nuggets were duly noted, for it was later when the fun would begin.

We were doing our stuff at a huge 'celeb' bash in Kensington in the summer of 1979. The client, a famous London figure with certain royal connections… was, in a word, up for it. I'd concoct rocket fuel cocktails that blew everyone's socks off and a few stilettoes too. As the guests started to sway, so we moved in like two prowling hyenas. I approached a well-known actor – indeed a household name.

"A drink sir?" I enquired politely. "Why, th-thank you, young man." He smiled. "My pleasure, sir." I replied, swapping his old glass for yet another lethal dose of pure white spirit. "I hope sir doesn't mind me mentioning something? I mean, one trusts you wouldn't be offended if I was to enquire about a certain something?"

"Oh... well... no, I suppose not," came the retort. "How can I help you, my man?"

I whispered in his ear, "Pardon me, sir, but I'm just interested to know, I mean it would be of some interest, how did your wife react when she found out you'd been giving the waitress at Tramp one up the arse?"

The reactions would range from explosive to nuclear, but emotions eventually cooled when the host, after a few treasured minutes of savouring the melee, came over to explain the prank. When the funny side eventually dawned, it was all pals together and by the end of the evening everyone was so wasted it was hard to determine the guests from the client, the door staff from the Dial-a-Waiters.

Fun was the order of the day and fun we had. As Kof would often comment, "That was a gig I will try to remember for a long time."

CHAPTER 18

It Was... Just Like That!

1980ish

One fine spring morning, I awoke in a creative mood.

What hero would I like to meet? Egad... my hero of heroes was Tommy Cooper. After a pinch of snowy snuff, I called Thames TV and got through to Mike Aspel's 'Six O'clock Show'.

"Hello," I chirped far too breezily. "My name is Steve Blacknell and I am president of the Tommy Cooper Fan Club of Great Britain. I see that Tom is playing at Windsor Blazers in a month or two and thought would it be okay if we all went to see him and film us all dressed as the great man!"

Four weeks later, dear Janet Street Porter was standing outside BBC Centre waiting to step onto a bus full of thirty highly-charged fans – all fizzed up and coked to the max. The ITV cameras then filmed the trip with us all doing TC impersonations and the gig itself – which I saw from under a table. I was laughing so hard and was so far gone it was impossible to stay in my seat. He was just out of this world.

He started the show in the same way as he had when my dad saw him in Margate in 1956.

"Ladies and Gentlemen," blared the MC, "Please welcome Mr Tommy Cooper!"

Nothing. Silence - then the funniest voice in show business broke the silence. "I'm in the dressing room," he shouted. "And I can't get out. I had the key but I can't get out!"

Titters turned to full blown manic laughter as he continued from backstage, and by the time he finally emerged from behind the curtain... the whole place was in total uproar. I was actually under the table in fits of amphetemine-ised giggles and could just make out his gargantuan size fourteen feet in huge black squeaky shoes coming towards me.

If genius is making people laugh without actually being there then Tommy Cooper was indeed that genius.

I do believe the record for this memorable stunt was some twenty-three minutes before he actually emerged to face the audience.

His stage farewell was, I'm told, yet another favourite of his.

"I gotta go now, I gotta make my way up the M1, I dunno why, I don't live up there!"

It was time to go and I was rounding up the remnants of the crew when I noted one of our number missing. I found my old Decca mate, Andre, outside Cooper's dressing room. "Back to the coach, quick," I shouted. As he scooted away, the dressing room door opened... and there he stood, the man-mountain of comedy himself, Tommy Cooper. "Come in, come in," he slurred. "Have a seat." I was dumbstruck. The buzzing in my bones stepped up a notch. Speechless.

I glanced back to the studio door where the coach with thirty of my best pals were all waiting for me... then I looked back at Cooper. 'Stuff 'em,' I thought. So, there I sat - face to face with my all-time hero. Tommy was now in shorts, dripping sweat on to the floor, a giant cigar in one hand and a whisky the size of Scotland in the other. He just grinned.

I am rarely stuck for words but I was flummoxed. In desperation I blurted, "So Tommy, we all came down to see you today, we're all from the music business, telly and like, the so-called youth of today. What do you think about the fact than WE think you are God?" Fixing his huge eyes on mine, he took a giant draw on the cigar, and as he exhaled a huge cloud, he tipped half of the glass past his cavernous lips and with a massive sigh exclaimed, "Do you know what? I think it's fucking amazing."

Well, that was it - there and then that seemed the funniest thing I had ever heard. He just sat there, silent, and the more I thought about it, the funnier it got. I fell to the floor, helpless. I was laughing so hard it hurt - oh God it hurt. Mumbling excuses, I thanked him and hared it to the coach. I laughed all the way back to London. I had met my God, only for a few minutes, but, in a weird way - just like seeing Hendrix a decade before - that had been enough.

One of the true creative geniuses of our times, and there'll never be another like him.

CHAPTER 19

The Screen on Winchmore Hill

1981...ish

By now, Maggie and I had become firm friends once more and my crazed meandering was now cast aside to history.

It's only in the last few years that it has indeed occurred to me what an utter bastard I've been to most of the lovely ladies who've adorned my life. A sobering thought to be sure amidst these random ramblings.

I'd made up my mind that I'd never treat her badly ever again. A vow I'd break yet again some years later when success came a knocking.

As she was temporarily bereft of male company, we decided to get a flat together and, for no reason I can recall, decided to join the likes of Cliff Richard, Keith Moon and Frank Ifield who'd all lived in the tree-friendly London suburb of Winchmore Hill, London N21.

Separate beds of course, but then that suited us perfectly. Amazing how we could switch our sexual instincts on and off like an alarm, but in truth I think I always fancied her. I was just a twat with the female species! As they say, if they sewed castanets on the inside of me trousers, I still couldn't click with the women for any period of time!

We'd come up with a very exciting ruse to entertain our mates. We called it The Screen on Winchmore Hill.

I'd black out the flat with curtains, don my Dial a Waiter suit and open the doors at 6.30pm prompt. The guests would pay two quid to sit in the very cramped lounge and sit through my opening speech - in my best Tony Hancock tones, "Welcome indeed to the Screen on Winchmore Hill, ladies and gentlemen."

It had all proved a massive success, and I would have bookings three months ahead!

It was midday on that fateful Saturday and with only two hours sleep under my belt and an anvil weighing heavy on my chest from the night before, I realised I had fifteen excitement-hungry devotees coming round later for the 'Screen'. There were bodies scattered everywhere from the night before with the odd stoned stalwarts still excitedly rolling spliffs and chopping out lines.

I was reminded too that four of the said survivors were staying on for the evening's entertainment, so I politely asked the remainder to think about getting their battle-scarred arses home and return later. To my joy and delight, I espied half a bottle of red wine some poor fool had forgotten to consume – and I was on it like an eagle on a bunny... trying to feel better and more in touch with planet Earth.

But as time wore on, so the worse was the feeling. I decided to panic about the evening. I felt like death. There was only one thing for it. Popeye had his spinach. Me? I had port and brandy! My trusty P&B had got me out of countless scrapes.

One time, years ago in Sheffield, I'd had a tummy upset from too much booze and a bulimia session the night before and had to get on a choo-choo to Edinburgh for lunch with a radio client. I was at the train station and the cab driver had told me about the magical merits of a Port and Brandy. It could turn the meek and mild into two separate gorillas. I knocked back two large ones in the pub next door and suddenly a zing went up my spine... I kid you not. Amazing. I boarded the train to Edinburgh a renewed man.

Later, over the border, I enjoyed a wonderful haggis lunch, which I kept down (by the way) accompanied by a gallon of red wine and a few whiskies to boot. Sheer magic. I'd very often meet similarly overhung chums for drinks, stride up to the bar and say "Two treble port and brandies, please?" My chum would say to the startled bar person, "And the same for me."

From feeling crap, to a happy chap, just add Port and Brandy! That most ebullient elixir's startling qualities can cure an upset tum in a trice, and in terms of instant buzz, drum up stark images of Clark Kent emerging from that phone booth, a refreshed and highly charged individual.

So, that Sunday back at Winchmore Hill, I glanced at the clock. "Oh, shit me pants, it's... it's nearly TWO O'CLOCK!" The bloody buggering offey shuts in three minutes. QUICK! Who can give me a lift?"

There followed a nervy, wobbly dash to said house of booze, just managing to catch my good pal, the ageing Mr Wincey, as he was putting up that dreaded closed sign that so carved terror into our hearts. I emerged beaming like a baby four minutes later - with two bottles each of Hine brandy and Cockburn's port. "Hoorah," I sang to myself. "The Screen will go ahead. HOORAH!"

By 5.30 I had downed, save a few drips, a bottle of each. My darling P&B. Oh you do so much for me! I was now ready to take on, not just the evening's audience, but everything in general. I was ready, willing, and able Mabel.

The bell rang prompt at 6.30 pm – the first three Screen members, livers and noses poised for action, had arrived. They were greeted by a bright red sign pinned to the front door. Scrawled in wibbly-wobbly, black felt tip were the immortal words, 'The Management of the Screen on Winchmore Hill would Like to Thank Hine Brandy and Cockburn's Port – Without Whom Tonight's Performance would not be Possible.'

The evening was of course a resounding success... with the wonderfully awful *'The Return of the Killer Tomatoes'* the surprise smash of the evening. The skimpily dressed guest hostess, 'Dolly' Brown, had also proved a hit, selling out of coke at 20p a line, joints at 2p a go, and the house special, one 'blue' – a particularly pacey little speed pill – and a hit of tequila for the once only bargain price of just 15p!

In retrospect this was really 'Sausage Part 2'. The unbridled joy of revelling in raucous, riotous behaviour in downbeat downtown suburbia. Sex, drugs and rolly rock just feet away from Mr and Mrs Normal next door only added to the thrill. Having such frivolities on a Sunday evening was, of course, bordering on the clinically insane with most of us working the next day, but it all seemed legitimate warfare at the time.

CHAPTER 20

I'm Glad 'I Ran'

1982...ish

I was now fully ensconced as an all-in-one PR/A&R chappie at the newly formed Jive Records in the yet to be trendy, somewhat downtrodden, district that was Willesden, North London and loved every second. I was out there in every sense of the word, going from gig to gig each and every night in search of the band that would make my name. Out there indeed with enough cocaine and my beloved port and brandy in my system to sink the Pilgrim Fathers.

One lazy hazy summer night I saw one of the worst dressed combos I had ever clapped my reading glasses on. They called themselves A Flock of Seagulls and they made me weep. One particular song sent my trusty arm hairs skywards. I knew this was a State-side smash and legged it back to the Jive boss, Clive Calder babbling about it being a top ten USA hit!

He duly signed them and nine months later *'I Ran'* stood loud and proud at number four in the USA charts.

It was two years later that the band had got a Grammy for Best Instrumental Performance for *'DNA'* from their self-titled debut album, and had sold out Radio City in NYC. I was MC. I came out to wild applause. "Now, I'm from England," I hooted, and the whole place exploded, everyone stood and applauded.

"So, now for the latest 'Fab Four' from Liverpool. Ladies and gentlemen...please welcome...A Flock of Seagulls!" Pandemonium! Ecstasy. A triumph!

Those moments don't come along very often, but when they do, you grab with both hands and enjoy each and every second. I ended up snogging the lead singer's girlfriend high up in the rafters. We galloped into the night and took the last train to Westport, Connecticut where we rocked and mainly rolled about for three long days and nights.

In truth I should have managed the band in those early days – but I really didn't have the experience. I often wish I had.

I still adore their music and am still in touch with drummer Ali and bassist Frank. Mike later went off to form his own 'spin off' outfit, but at least he's kept the band name alive

They may have been castigated by the ever-lethal UK press calling them 'A Flock of Haircuts', but after conquering the USA, Canada, Australia etc. who gave a flying fucklet!

I'm still chuffed that when '*I Ran*' back to the Jive boss, I knew I was onto something!

It's great being right – as long as you can forget the times you're wrong! Selective memory is a wonderful thing.

CHAPTER 21

Food, Food – Unglorious Food!

1980ish

Although a golden boy in the work place, privately I was descending to hitherto unseen depths of despair. I was now a full-blown anorexic bulimic. It had taken over my life and I was in real shit. I had no idea exactly why this was all happening. I just felt lonely, as if there was a hole in my heart that needed repair. But I had no idea how to mend it!

I was now starving myself from Friday through to Monday so I could look jolly nice and thin for everyone the following week.

I was existing on a bizarre and barren diet of black coffee, speed, ladies' menstrual pills that made you pee like a garden hose, and barrel loads of diet coke. My mind was totally shattered. My addictive juices were over-flowing and substance abuse was spiralling into free-fall.

A cold, wet Monday morning in Willesden sure took some beating. Invariably when the weekly meeting was over, I would find myself fleeing the Jive HQ as if some crazed satanic 'Sat Nav' was perched on my shoulder. As if possessed, I would shamble along the High Road and find myself in my favourite mini-market.

After three days of total denial, I wanted to eat the world, and everybody in it. Into the magic basket it would all fly - pork pies, Cadbury's tinned sponges (a particular favourite eaten raw), crisps, éclairs, baked beans... and chocolate. One of everything. And coke. No diet stuff THIS time baby. The real thing. The sweeter and sicklier the better. A short hop to my favourite park bench and down it would all go. Enough food to sustain the average Joe and Jolene for a week. In a flash. In a second. Hardly touched the sides. Like a gannet gulping a big fish.

No crunch - no munch. Just a steady procession of bulky junk, one crammed mouthful after another. Once my bag was empty it was as if I started to 'come to'. The spell was broken.

Then, ‘quick SB, dump the bags in the waste bin and back to the office’.

Only one sad and lonely destination in mind. The staff loo. It would take about ten minutes to cough it all up with maybe six or so thrusts of the well-honed two fingered action I knew so well. A few sprays of mouth spray from my bag, a brush of the old toothypegs, a few extra-strong mints, and I was good to go.

Lunch would then be a few pints in the local, and a few port and brandies to settle the stomach. My poor old stomach.

Although I was a fucking mess, I had a very different burning in my guts. I was now beginning to tire of my job promoting everybody else except me. I still had this belief buried in the depths of my bowels that I had something to say to the world. I had not a clue what the hell it was, but something stirred within. However, I had to be honest - I was on the downward slope, and had begun to drown my sorrows in rivers of bourbon and mountains of pills. On the outside, pretty and pencil-thin, a happening bunny, but on the inside, with Maggie having flown the coop for the delights of Wandsworth Common, I felt fat and very alone.

CHAPTER 22

Down by the Riverside

1981

I had now purchased my first flat in downtown Hornsey and would sit there on my red-ragged sofa for days on end in between food binges.

Through the BBC bushwire I'd heard they were auditioning for presenters for a brand-new alternative rock show, '*Riverside*' that would come from The Whistle Test office - with none other than the great man himself, Michael Appleton, at the helm.

"There's no way we are having any record promo people involved", he yelled at me down the phone one Monday morning. "So, you can forget it – but you're welcome to come along in your waiter's uniform and be interviewed as we know you'll never shut up!" So that's what I did, and he was right – I kept talking and talking. As I left the studio, I'll never forget him yelling, "We weren't meant to be looking at you!"

I had a letter a few weeks later saying I could do a few shows for them as a trial and see how it went.

The shows creator and producer, John Burrowes, called me. "Okay - against all logic we are giving you a chance. If you mess up, I will visit you and personally kick your head in. Good luck."

The next day I was all set to quit my job at Jive. I was just about to call upstairs to the boss and tell him that I wanted to give TV stardom a shot, but as I picked up the phone, so my phone rang. It was Clive's secretary. "He'd like to see you in twenty minutes," she said.

"I really am sorry but I have to let you go Steve," he said in his own officious South African nasal tones. "No room for you. But we can't thank you enough."

By way of a thank you I ended up going over to the USA with the Seagulls as their MC and had the time of my life.

So - we were 'live' on Jan 1st, 1982. I was opening BBC 2's 'hip' new pop fashion show *'Riverside'* with a link into a brand-new band we had on the show - New Order!

The audience? A make-up box on legs, including a pretty young chappie calling himself Boy George, desperate to get on the show (I believe George once said *Riverside* was the only show where you had to audition the audience), but, as he was obviously heading for obscurity why bother booking him? Even though we were billed as an 'outrageous' YOOF show, both George and Frankie Goes to Hollywood never made the line-up – so that's why *'The Tube'* nabbed them!

Aside from "Hey there, you big fat twat," the worst thing you can tell an anorexic bulimic is 'Did you know that TV puts eight pounds on you?' You may just as well have pushed me under a 96 bus. But no. It was true – it bloody did!

I had starved for three days in a brave and determined attempt to look as waif-like as possible for my TV debut. I had even cut down on the booze. A somewhat dramatic course – but every calorie counted. I was 'live' to the nation at 7.30pm. I had my five lines on autocue, all set - but inside I was a total wreck.

After dress rehearsal it was time for the cast and crew to have a snack. I glared at the endless assortment of cakes, croissants and finger food before me. I suddenly felt the hunger. Gingerly I picked up a salmon sandwich and some crisps and a bun and retired to the refuge of my dressing room to stuff my face, far away from the madding crowd.

Five minutes later I was throwing it all up. Every bit. I had a huge line to perk me up a tad, adjust the mascara, a fiddle with the frilly collar and I looked just fab baby!

My poor tum was throbbing. My throat too, but when the time came that night... when I spoke to the nation, all the words were in the correct order.

Later that night I sat expectantly parked on my sofa as I whizzed back the video to see how thin and wonderful I had been. In my haste I had recorded *Coronation St.* instead. My pager lay as quiet as a dead mouse. The phone too. 'Welcome to show business', I thought. Hoo fucking RAH!

I'd hit the screen at a very good time. I was nearing thirty. Brash... speedy... and with an androgynous look of the day that would serve my career well. To some people I WAS the

80s. I had a credible fan base, knew every bugger on the scene and would go to the opening of a bleeding envelope.

In keeping with my new found B list fame, I systematically began to get rid of everyone around me who did not walk the showbiz way. Now I had the smell of money in what remained of my nose, and there was not a moment to lose.

WHAT A TWAT!

CHAPTER 23

Here Comes the Night Nosher

1981

Maggie and I were now together in yet another flat in super trendy Hampstead Garden Suburb

By now I had reasoned that being pals was the way forward as 1: Sex tends to complicate things, and 2: she didn't fancy me anymore. Anytime she dated someone I could feel this weird jealous feeling creeping up my spine, yet deep inside I knew I deserved everything I got!

She was, though, a good listener and loved a good debate, so I was able to pour out my addiction woes to her, which I now see as the beginning of me coming to terms with it all. The three-four-day fasts continued in earnest – but now with a bizarre nocturnal twist.

I had started to sleep eat!

My system was getting a little pissy with me. Most unreasonably it was now demanding some morsels of goodness that could hopefully stay down and supply the odd shred of nourishment. So it was that, along with my daylight fasts, I now began to dance and dabble with the nocturnal nosebag! Historically I would deny my body solids throughout the day, but often beg her to rope my feet up to the end of the bed with several cans of diet coke by my bedside so I couldn't wander – searching for nourishment in my sleep. And not just the odd salt and vinegar crisp either!

I began to cook in my sleep.

I can vaguely recall the first time it happened. It was about three in the morning, and Maggie had been awakened by a scuffling and clinking noise in the kitchen. Bleary-eyed, she poked her head around the door to find yours fucking truly fiercely embroiled in making a marmite omelette. I can still recall her, somewhat pensive, "Steve, are you okay?" I awoke like an athlete from the blocks. "Whaaa...? Wass up?" I enquired, as I stared down before me at a fully-fledged meal in progress. My body was playing catch up - and my brain was still between the sheets.

This whole night-feast thing gradually escalated into a full-blown culinary farce. Sometimes, I actually got to the eating bit before she would wake me. Sometimes she would just let me get on with it – as deep inside she knew this was the only nutrients my body would get until the following night! Although we'd later laugh about it over a drink, it was agreed to attempt to nip these peculiar goings-on in the bud in the sincere hope that we might address the daytime issue with a clean slate.

She bought a padlock. A big bugger.

On paper it sounded a top ruse – the ropes had been a distinct failure as I'd always manage to untie them, she would go to bed with the keys and in the event that I would be denied access to the kitchen - the jolt might well awaken me and nudge me back to beddy-byes. In theory, a good idea.

A devout and hardened 'veggie' she had spent ages making one of her favourite meals - a garlic lentil stew. A bucket of it and I could smell that it must have tasted good.

However, the thought of eating with daylight all around, the very IDEA of looking less than sparrow-slim was all too much, so as usual I declined dinner and stuck to a bottle or two of fine red wine. Much better for you. I was like some weird crazed culinary vampire.

It must have been about 4.30 the next morning, and it was no surprise for her to hear noises emanating from the direction of the kitchen. But, turning on the hall light, I was nowhere to be seen. She could just make out some heaving and grunting noises emanating from the lounge. She gently pushed open the door to see a pair of windsock-white legs dangling from the serving hatch. I was stuck in my sleep.

She opened the kitchen door to find my head dangling over the remains of the lentil stew scooping huge spoonfuls into my mouth. She told me the next day that she had just left me there as it all looked too dangerous a scenario to attempt to break my spell.

On reflection I guess she got that right. Even old chirpy bollocks here would have found it hard to explain exactly why one was wedged in a hatch in the middle of the night scooping last night's din-dins into a gaping gob!

It's so clear to me now that my subconscious mind had mentally noted where she had left the wretched concoction on the bench just below the hatch, and in my state of oblivion, the 'chef of darkness' was homing in on some sustenance. The next morning the bowl was empty, I awoke with hardened blobs of brown stew down my T-shirt, and I was sick as a dog.

One last crack at it we thought. Another padlock for the hatch itself. That MUST do it. But alas, she would often wake to find me staring at her, Rasputin-like, at the bottom of her bed... pleading for the keys to the kitchen.

In the end she surrendered, and so, every night, I took the keys to bed, woke up, oblivious of all around me - let myself into the kitchen, ate whatever was in the fridge – or maybe knocked up a nice cheese toastie or as I did one time embark upon the preliminary stages of a vegetable and fish pie. I would then let myself out, lock up and go back to a slumber of sorts.

Unfortunately, this nocturnal noshing was not merely confined to my own four walls. I would continue my night-time travels when staying at other people houses too. Talented huh?

One time I was staying at my little Godson's rather posh house in Kensington as it was his birthday the next day. When his mother went to the fridge to cook his morning boiled egg, her thirty-five quid cake was gone and, in its place sat a pile of crumbs and some half-chewed iced figures. I had even eaten the candied hand-drawn birthday message.

The 'galloping shitting gourmet' had been at it again!

I ran out into Gloucester Road and bought a replacement for a fiver. I apologised for weeks on end, but how can you explain to a five-year-old and a pissed off mother that Uncle Stephen had unceremoniously scoffed his birthday cake in his sleep. The answer is, you can't, which is precisely what I think she called me when she went to the fridge that morning.

Oops!

CHAPTER 24

And Nothing but the Tooth

1981

My androgynous looks were working a treat in the lady's department, and I got bolder by the day in my quest to date the rich and famous. Whilst taking part in a Radio One Trivia marathon, I espied a young lady who I instantly clocked was the wondrous Kit Hain – she of Marshall Hain – '*Dancing in the City*'. I was a fan. Before long we were an item, and I was dancing on air!

Besides being famous and sexy, Kit was a FUNNY lady, a real comic and would do the best Janet Street Porter impression. After the Cooper trip, Janet and I had got to know each other – she was going out with Tony from ZZ Sputnik, who I knew – and I had just guested on her '*Network 7*' YOOF show on Channel 4.

Kit would often call me in character.

"Hullo Shtoive – Janet here... why don't I come round there tonight and give you a right good seeing to!" Then, it would get graphic and we would collapse in separate heaps.

One Monday morning, the house phone woke me from too little sleep.

"Hello Shtoive – it's Janet here." I was half awake.

"Why don't you fuck off, you bucked tooth c**t," I heard myself say

Silence. And as the silence developed into a deathly one, it gradually dawned on me the whole enormity and possibility of what I had done hit me like a sledgehammer.

"Hello... er... Janet?" I murmured, "Hello?"

With a tut – the line went dead.

I never spoke to her again for 32 years until I met her at a media do... I tapped her on the shoulder in the interval... "Oh, it's yoo!" She tutted once more and walked off.

Can't really say I blame her either!

CHAPTER 25

Breakfast Anyone?

After calling the Deputy Editor of BBC *Breakfast Time* most days for about six weeks, I was drafted in to do the pop news when the late Mike Smith had fortuitously for me come down with a very bad flu bug. Lino Ferrari more or less repeated word for word what John B. had told me a year before. "This is your chance, Blacknell. Don't fuck up."

I stayed for three years and learned my trade from the nation's favourite nice guy, Frank Bough. He was just wonderful to be with, both on and off camera. Little did I know that, deep down, cuddly Uncle Frank was a thrill-seeker too.

He was an out and out sex seeker, and many stories still exist about his antics in Broadcasting House and beyond.

But I can talk. I looked like I'd failed the audition for The Tiller Girls and was hardly a role model for aspiring young presenters.

With seconds to go before we went live, he would be muttering into my ear all manner of dodgy stuff about what had happened the night before with members of the opposite sex. The Gallery would be counting him down. "Okay, Frank, we are live in 5-4-3..." and as the last word left his lips - normally something a bit naughty - he would glide effortlessly into host mode, right on cue. "And good morning, everyone, today our guests include 'Mr Winston Madaggala', the Ugandan Minister for Sport - and now over to you Selina."

I'll never forget the first bit of advice he gave me. "Steve, if you want to sleep with anybody on this show, don't bother with the producer or the director. Head for that person there – autocue – ALWAYS remember their name. It's they who can make and break careers."

Great advice from one of the best. A scholar and a gentleman. I have a lot to thank Frank for.

Business wise, I was pretty spot on. I was likeable, reliable mostly, and easy to work with. Life was good and lunch was invariably in the West End at some swanky top person's restaurant.

Then of course, there was cocaine, lots and lots of cocaine, blowing in like snow flurries from *'Dr Zhivago'*.

But there was cleaner living too. Some nights I'd go on to Tramp nightclub for a gentle vodka and chips with me old mucker Bill Wyman and assorted cohorts, with pints of bitter with the lovely Les Dawson, Eddie Kidd or Jim Davidson at Stringfellows - hell, it was the 80s! Other nights I'd blur the evening and morning away until the small hours. Then, around 5.30am, another car to ferry me to Television Centre, where I would pop up, unfeasibly bright-eyed, to greet the nation as they tucked into their porridge and bacon. I must be the only presenter in TV history to have his make-up taken OFF to go on the telly!

Also, seemingly part of the gig was to ignore the non-famous around me i.e. folk and friends I had known for donkey's years, preferring to mix with fellow 'B' list celebs. I would knock around with the likes of Rory Bremner, Carol Vorderman, etc. – and not really have time to see my real mates.

Although I'd been a wreck inside, on the outside I looked the part. Pencil-thin, speedy and up for anything and everything.

It was, in all truth, amazing that girls fancied me with my androgynous girly look, make-up, cape and black ski pants. Although I wasn't exactly the 80s Russell Brand, I still managed to bed a fair bevy of tip top talent.

For some unaccountable reason, I had quite a thing for weather-girls, including the lovely ITV presenter Trish Williamson. We had a good thing going but it all went very pear shaped when she insisted she was pregnant, and it all got very messy and complicated. We were soon finished as an item, and I found out from the private doctor I'd sent her to that it was all phoney.

She sadly died in a car crash in 2007. A lovely lady. It was such a tragedy.

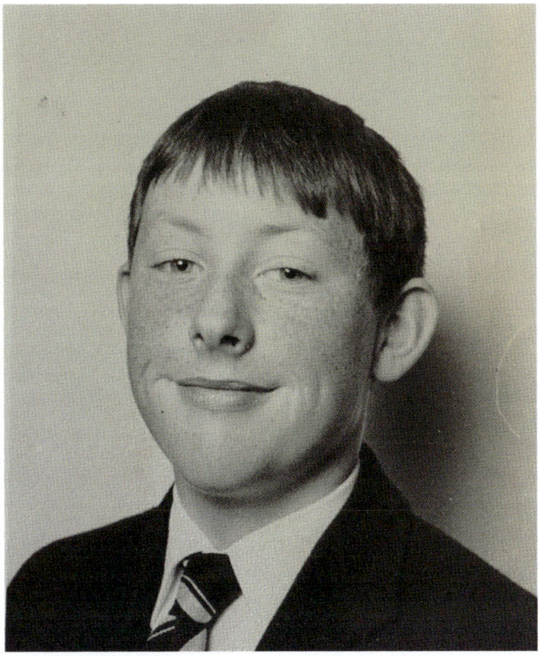

Innocent daze. The future pop pundit

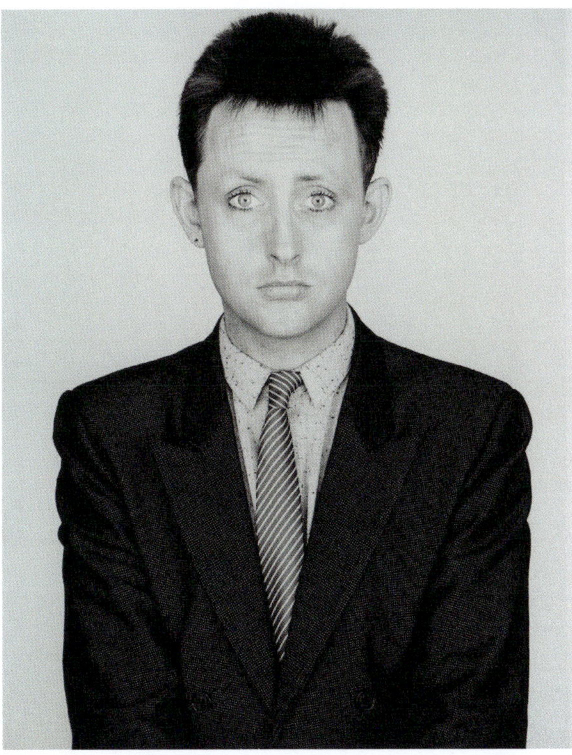

'Pretty on the outside' but sick with Bulimia on the inside

Me with Sooty and my hero of heroes, Robin Williamson

At the BBC with that rascally rat

With 'Whispering' Bob Harris

Maggie and her 'Dial a Waiter'

A lovely day in Tinseltown with a bedroom wall hero, Dudley Moore

Terminally hip record exec before my clothes shrunk

How to smile and talk about pubic hair at the same time

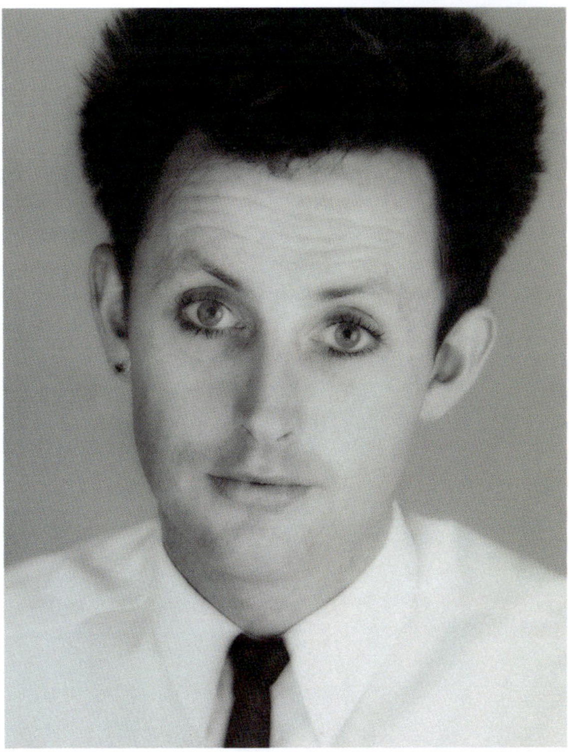

More make-up than Dusty Bloody Springfield!

With Ms Bush in groovy downtown Dartford

My Knock your Block Off PR shoot

If you want the stories, I've got 'em all. My name's Steve Blacknell and I'm 'Off The Wall'

Sooty grooving to Hendrix on Brighton beach

Me? Gay?

With my 'silver lady'

Kicking off my 'Moody' boots

Yippee, I'm a Hippee!

Gary Numan easing my fears

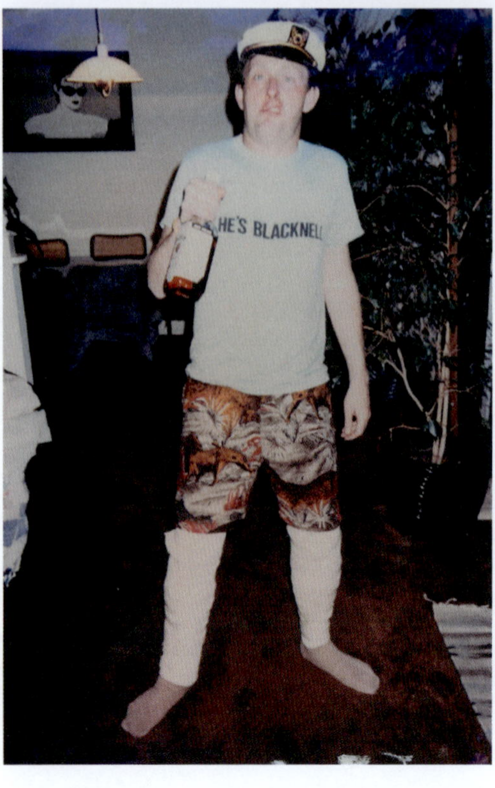

What remained of me after being blown up in Marina Del Ray

Boy meets curl

Ho bleedin' Ho

A close shave with Frank Sidebottom and pal

In Sight, in Sound and in Concert

CHAPTER 25 ½

To Be Frank

You may or may not recall, but as a new decade dawned, so 1980 saw the extraordinary *'I'm In Love with The Girl on a Certain Manchester Megastore Checkout Desk'*. The band clocking up their solitary UK hit were The Freshies and the somewhat eccentric lead singer was a certain Chris Sievey.

Chris was a total fucking genius and had invented a fictional character called Frank Sidebottom.

Frank was a besuited wide-eyed 'live' cartoon figure with papier-mâché head and, with the addition of a swimming peg pinned to his nose, he became a walking talking nasal catastrophe.

He WAS Frank!

Chris and I would often meet in his favourite Manchester drinking haunts and plot world domination. He was stuffed full of weird and wonderful ideas, and I, like many, was lost in admiration.

As if that wasn't enough silliness he also had 'Little Frank' and an even dafter 'Amoeba Frank' as his sidekicks, and he soon became a cult hero to the rock and rollers whilst winning over the children's TV audience with many an appearance on prime time kids shows.

I could go on and on about his array of skills – he was also an incredible cartoonist who would just ooze with originality and outrageous ideas.

I became his 'go to' MC and would regularly introduce 'Frank' events. In fact, I worked so much with him that there were rumours that I was the man in the mask, something that I was very chuffed with.

It was indeed part of the game. WHO was Frank?

I was hosting a gig at London's Rock Garden in Covent Garden one time and Frank – complete with trademark banjo - had just finished his act and strode off to tumultuous applause.

Now minus head, Chris joined me in the crowd as they were yelling "More, more!"

As we clapped furiously together, he turned to me… "Isn't this fucking great Blacknell!"

What a man!

Another time I had him as a surprise guest on my BBC *Breakfast Time* pop slot. I had told the 'gallery' to make sure they got a close-up ready on dear Frank Bough who had no clue what was going to happen.

As the tinkling of a bell rang offstage, so on came Frank atop a very boyish bicycle… and parked it by the legendary sofa.

"SNAP," he said to an astonished Boughy… "What?" Frank said. "SNAP… Frank and Frank!"

The look on our hosts face was pure magic.

"So, who is this, Steve?" he enquired. "Well, this is Frank Sidebottom," I replied, "And he's a famous musician."

"Yes," retorted Sidebottom. "And my new record is number one in the Timperley charts." (Timperley was Frank's native home district in Greater Manchester – a fact he would ram home at every opportunity).

As if by magic and with no prompting, Bough said, "The Timperley chart? Well, who compiles it?"

"I do," chimed Frank. "Straight in at number one!"

There followed a deathly silence then you could hear the fellow hosts and crew alike rattling with laughter.

Most of his record releases were first degree murder adaptations of big hits… and when Chris called me to ask if I'd guest star in the video of Frank's horrendous new version of a Wings classic titled 'Mull of Timperley'… I accepted with relish.

It was shot in the back garden of a house in Maidstone, Kent. It featured yours truly as the homeowner who was shaving, only to see Frank and his band (containing BBC broadcaster Mark Radcliffe accompanied by Little Frank) swaying around in theatrical smoke – completely dismantling another pop classic

It's on YouTube – take a lookee.

So that was Frank and that was Chris who passed away in June of 2010. A genius who left us all too soon.

But Sidebottom still lives in the minds of those who loved and admired his beautifully bizarre take on life.

And what a life!

CHAPTER 26

Needle Time

My dearest pal, Kof, had just passed away from a dreadful brain tumour, weirdly enough while watching *The Blues Brothers* - this was a terrible blow. Although we had parted, the lovely Kit told me all about her chum who'd tried Traditional Chinese Acupuncture as a means to counter any upset and bring about 'a sense of balance to mind and body'.

Never one to shirk the idea of something new, on her recommendation, I contacted a lady called Carol in the far-flung borders of Cambridge.

This particular school of acupuncture dwelt on the spiritual side of life – aside from the more medical approaches of other more 'Western' methods, and as an apprentice Buddhist and eternal dippy Hippy, it was right up my ethereal alley!

It consisted of hourly appointments with at least half the duration spent chatting away about one's innermost thoughts, apprehensions, hopes, and fears. In my case I was in little bits over my recent loss and it really helped to talk about it all to someone trained to listen... and more importantly never, ever to judge!

Now knee deep in cash, I was able to go once a week and it became a welcome diversion from all the media shit I was now immersed in.

After a few visits with the diminutive yet delightful Carol, I began to feel much better in myself. In truth, just as in any form of therapy, the more you give the more you get in return, and being blessed as a communicative sort I welcomed the chance to blurt about myself.

It wasn't long before my various addiction problems emerged as a topic of conversation, and although I had a hold of the booze and drug problems, my food issues were now literally eating away at any goodness that remained in my system.

I'd had to come to terms with the fact that I was terribly ill. With the constant expulsion of bodily electrolytes and general disregard for my battered digestive system, I was heading headlong for what could be a terminal tumble.

Gradually, without realising it, I was opening up about the seeds being sown and the subsequent triggers that had taken over my waking life – and indeed my subconscious world too.

As I've mentioned, my own theory on addiction has always centred on the 'hole in the heart' idea. A hole to be filled, a gap to be bridged, and somehow, and I'll never know how, I began to feel a sense of well-being. Indeed, I started to buzz with life itself, and within three months I had stopped the self-abuse and had started to eat normally once more.

I was to binge only twice more. I've mentioned the 'Live Aid' occurrence but if I may - a quick diversion.

Through my appearance on BBC *Breakfast Time* when I'd 'come out' about my eating disorders, I'd been contacted by a lovely lady called Caroline who was a poor little thing... immersed in food problems way more dramatic than my situation.

Due to an appalling childhood with parental abuse so shocking I'll refrain from mentioning the details here, she defined the acute anorexic bulimic – and was always hovering around the five stone mark.

Both her great pal Judy and I tried our level best to help her but she'd always maintain that her condition was indeed 'all she had' and to take that away would leave her with nothing.

We arranged 'lunch' at a restaurant in her home town of Brighton. I had been 'clean' for around a year but approached the meet with some trepidation... knowing that it meant her having to eat something!

Enough to say that as we emerged from the restaurant, she yelled a huge, "YESSSSS."

It transpired that she'd eaten two lettuce leaves and kept them down! Hard to comprehend, I realised there and then that my illness had only really skimmed the surface of that terrible disease.

I'd often had the strangest feeling when I'd been in the presence of other sufferers... that in truth felt I could tell an anorexic from a few feet away. It was a 'vibe' that spelt unrest and a disturbed unhappy spirit.

I was getting a train back into London and on to acupuncture in Cambridge – and as we bade farewell - suddenly out of nowhere a familiar surge struck me like a thunderbolt.

I felt totally out of control, and in a scene reminiscent of the bad old days found myself in a bakery right next to the station. The next thing I knew I was aboard with two carrier bags brimming with squidgy cakes, buns, eclairs, and a giant plastic bottle of Pepsi.

Within ten or fifteen minutes the entire contents were consumed. Not chewed… swallowed. In another ten minutes or so I found myself in the toilet and down it went like a doughy, sickly waterfall of muck.

Shocked, I took my seat and trembled like a leaf the entire journey.

Talking with 'my needles lady' later that day I could only conclude that I'd picked up on her namesakes' 'vibe'. In other words, maybe just like any other addiction, the condition lies dormant until triggered.

As I always say when I lecture on the subject, I'm no expert, I just know what happened to me, but I'm lucky that I'm an open book and could open my heart too when it needed a chat.

Dear, sweet, lovely Caroline passed away a few months later.

Physically there was nothing of her, but she left behind a million smiles and I've always had the hope she went on to find a body she liked. Bless her.

CHAPTER 27

The Idiot Strikes Again!

By now Maggie was with a new love by the name of Raymond, and me with mine – the wonderful bluey/green eyed beauty that was Sonja.

I'd become a die-hard fan of the prog-rock monsters that were Marillion and had even been featured in their *'Heart of Lothian'* video along with the illustrious John Otway and Glyn Edwards of 'Minder' fame.

Sonja or 'Sonj', as she was affectionately called, was the sister of Suzie who was married to Mark, the band's keyboard player, and she was a complete darling. We now shared a second floor flat in Shepherd's Bush, 18 Stowe Road in fact. Just a stumble away from the BBC right around the corner.

My career was going from strength to strength and I was now guesting on a slew of BBC kids' shows. One such was *'Lift Off'* helmed by the genius of one Judy Whitfield, a wonderful exec who seemed to take me into her heart.

"We've a new band from Norway that I like, and I'd like you to interview them. It'll be their first UK appearance," she announced one day at a TV Centre meet.

It transpired that the three young hopefuls and a TV crew would join me in my front room the following Wednesday afternoon. And so it was that I and the virginal trio that were AHA, spent the afternoon drinking tea and talking *'Take on Me'*. I remember them now as real gents, and probably the best-looking blokes I'd ever met. The bastards.

There was a very funny time when they were doing a 'PA' at the HMV shop in Oxford Street, and I was there to chat to them. Funnily enough Maggie was with me that day as we turned up in a cab to see hundreds of screaming kids herding outside. I was so up myself by now I was convinced they were there to see me too and even Maggie looked impressed to say the least.

It was only after my quick chat with the boys that when they made their rapid exit, Maggie and I were left alone, with me, microphone in hand and a quizzical look on my pancake make-upped face that all became apparent. She laughed so hard I thought she'd pop. It took me a little longer to see the funny side but, eventually, I saw it too.

Just as Maggie and I had been so very happy all those years ago, Sonj and I were in total bliss, and as I was earning good money, I loved spoiling her. I'd treat her to the very best I could - clothes, the best food, champagne by the bucket full. Little did I know that I was sowing yet another seed of doom.

Although my bulimia was 'over', it was, in truth, always at arms-length and I really had no idea that what lay deep down in me would lead me to treat yet another lovely lady of mine so very, very badly. It was beginning to occur to me that my good lady was piling on the pounds - the good life that I'd given her was beginning to show - and although I tried, I could not get this out of my perpetually screwed up head. It eventually resulted in me giving her the unceremonious boot one Saturday. I knew it was wrong but the thought of anyone or anything less than thinly thin around me made me feel just downright awful. She went on to marry and have a lovely family. She was and is one of the best people I ever met, and has forgiven me my ignorant and hurtful ways.

But I'd done it again - just when things were going great, I'd pull it all out from under me. What a first-class idiot I really was.

I remember being on my own in the flat for many miserable months. Then, one Saturday in particular, eating enough dope cake to sink a fleet, I sat, unable to move. I stayed there for three days, save for several snail-like forays to the bog, and to the fridge for sod knows what I ate. I hated myself.

I still feel dreadful about what I'd done. And quite rightly so.

Maybe I should have titled this book, 'How to be a Twat and Get Away with It'.

CHAPTER 28

Trouble With a Fish and a Blancmange 1983

With my regular BBC TV work stacking up, I was now a regular host on Radio One's *'In Concert'* and also the simulcast with BBC2, *'Sight and Sound in Concert'* - I was seemingly everywhere at once!

Although I was now working, I somehow claimed the dole, and was only caught out when a DSS chap saw me on the telly and paid me a visit.

Great days, though, with 'Bring A Baked Potato' parties and the like.

I used to get visits from a tussly haired muso calling himself Dave Stewart.

He'd heard me on the radio and would either knock or slide cassettes through my letter box with notes.

He lived or worked around the corner, in a church I think, and was championing the vocal talents of one Annie Lennox.

I'd listen to them, but it would brush over me somewhat. I never got it.

I was later covering an awards show in London for MTV USA and had to interview them. The look in Dave's eyes said it all. To put it mildly he was a bit short, and whenever I interviewed him again, especially when he was with his then music partner, Feargal Sharkey, they were awkward to say the least!

Mind you, I can't blame Dave to be honest as I didn't recognise that particular genius.

I recall Annie was just lovely and I got on well with her mum!

For the *'In Concert'*, I'd been paid the princely sum of £40 – which covered doing the gig on a Wednesday night at London's Parish Theatre and a promo trailer on a Monday. Dear John Peel had just got the fee raised to that princely sum too! The BBC pay was crap until you got into the upper echelons, which I never managed to do. However, I was well on my way to being what is now a millionaire, earning £300k a year - easy-peasy -

without being a household name like Domestos or Fairy Liquid.

The producer of *'In Concert'* was the persona that was Jeff Griffin, a seasoned warhorse of BBC Radio – a cuddly grump of a man with a wit that could cut glass. He once described me as the only man he knew who wore make-up on the radio. Which indeed I did, tons of it.

Meanwhile, the *'Sight and Sound in Concert'* simulcast would come from a variety of venues from Chippenham's Gold Diggers to The Regal Theatre in Hitchin – with a variety of bands of the day. One such were my beloved Marillion, with their formidable frontman, Fish.

Perched on my stage spot one August night in front of a packed Chippenham crowd, we were going 'live' on TV and radio and, as I got the okay in the earpiece, I started to do my piece to camera when I could feel something solid under my throat. There, in full Fish multi-coloured warrior make-up was the man himself, simulating slitting my throat as I struggled to speak. Much merriment followed later that night with an abundance of the band's signature beverage, 'Grendel' – a chaotic cocktail of rum, advocaat, vodka, crème de menthe and more – much more – that the band had adopted early on in their checkered career.

Suffice to say that at the post-gig party, after we'd quaffed gallons of the stuff, a few fire extinguishers were let off and the rest is a blur. I vaguely remember waking up next morning with Fish next to me.

We became great mates from then on.

All good clean fun I have to say and again a night to try and remember!

My first ever live outside broadcast had been at the Regal a few years previously when I had to introduce 10 CC to a waiting nation. For weeks I had been walking around town rehearsing "Welcome to The Regal Theatre, Hitchin – here's Ten CC." I'd repeat it in the bath, in the cab, on the bog... a zillion times. When the day came, I was, of course, shitting myself as I heard "Action!" in my ear. Firmly, deliberately, and with complete confidence I uttered, "Welcome to the Hegal Theatre, Ritchen - here's ten cee cee!" As the band started to play, I could feel that any career I'd ever had was now slipping away into eternal hell. I felt the touch of tears in my eyes... it was over before it had really started. But nobody cared... the team thought it very funny, and it was forgotten immediately. I'd learned a very important lesson - when you're 'live' you can be forgiven most things, just never swear or be sexist or homophobic and you'll be okay.

The other gig that sticks in what's left of my mind was when that dapper duo, Blancmange, were our guests on 'Sight and Sound'.

Just before I was due to step onto my mark to rehearse the intro, Michael Appleton's voice rang out from the outside the broadcast truck. "Steve, please can you take your mark on that metal plate?" Looking down, I duly did as I was told. Going live, I started to deliver my intro perched on this sodding plate. As I was concluding my spiel, "Please welcome to Sight and Sound and in concert - it's ..." I failed to deliver that last line as at that precise moment, Tom Corcoran – Michael's long-time director and one of the funniest drunks and loveliest people you'd ever care to meet - rushed toward me and slapped a huge gooey blancmange in my face. As I wiped the sticky mess from my eye sockets, I just managed to shout 'BLANCMANGE!" Cue band. Cue hysterics from the truck.

I gathered from them later that the plate I stood on was there to prevent me being electrocuted. Bastards.

Mind you, the best ever trick played on me was in Amsterdam in 1993.

When I was filming on location with Cathay Pacific Airways, I had to do a piece to camera then turn and walk away – still jabbering on. Well, there's a rule in telly, you never, ever stop talking / walking until you hear the word "CUT!" I'd delivered my lines, turned, and kept walking and walking... still nothing. I'd covered quite a distance when I finally turned around, they were nowhere to be seen! The bastards had legged it in the truck and gone back to the hotel. Fortuitously I had some local currency on me and eventually got a cab back to base. They were all waiting for me in the bar – grinning from head to feet.

UTTER BASTARDS!

CHAPTER 29

Making Up And Raking It In

I'd now taken the plunge and bought a super trendy mansion flat in the even trendier Holland Park Avenue.

While my BBC activities and night owl lifestyle as Peter Stringfellows PR man were keeping me not only active but full to bursting at the bank, the thirst for more raged within. Money breeds money and the cash trees were in full blossom.

I spent three years working for him in the early eighties and would often stay up late, late drinking with the likes of Les Dawson and me old mucker Eddie Kidd.

Peter was a strange and endearingly delightful man, and I loved my evenings there and it was his girlfriend, Frizzby Fox and I who opened his then latest venture The Hippodrome in Leicester Square.

On a cultural level the effect of the 'New Romance' with Boy George at the helm was huge!

Boys now looked like girls with outrageous make-up and fashion to match... bell sleeves, silver accessories and wide boots – it was all or nothing. It was in truth a time where music *followed* fashion with many an artist 'storyboarding' a video and then composing a tune around it!

I relished this dramatic quantum leap as I'd never seen myself as a 'blokes' bloke' as exemplified by my constant quest to be thin and lovely which was reaching its height around this time. I recall the late great and supremely gay Kenny Everett telling me 'I was a bit of a let-down to my parents... they wanted me to be a big hairy thing like me dad!".

I began to wear more and more make-up to see what I could get away with and by the time I arrived at the BBC Breakfast Time sofa in '83. I resembled 'Dusty Springfield on acid' according to one of the floor managers!

I fucking loved it

Typifying my addictive bent I tried to take things to their illogical extreme, experimenting with girly clothes both at home and in public. Normality sucked and I was going hell for handkerchief whatever that means.

So, with pound notes spurting out of every aperture in a fit of acute boredom, one day I called a clinic in London to see how much a sex-change would cost.

Just like the Lighthouse idea a decade earlier, it seemed a good idea at the time.

Suffice to say and to state the bleeding obvious I took it no further, but old habits die hard and truth be told I've not been out of any of my houses without make-up of some sort ever since. Sometimes people have a pop at me but A. What's wrong with looking good, and B. I don't give a shit anyway.

Note: Over the last six years I've also had a few 'non-invasive' facial procedures including the 'Vampire Facelift' where they take blood, separate it and inject your face with the white cells... in effect your 'DNA'. The resulting bruising is dramatic to say the least and I have to say I get very disappointed if people don't remark on it. Narcissist me? Nah... no way!

I rest my case M'Lud and ask for fifteen other ridiculous actions to be taken into consideration.

Voice work had become a steady earner... bearing in mind that in them there 1980s money was splashed about like dishwater. Because of my TV antics, I started to become in demand for 'shout overs' as we called them.

I was hired as the voice of HMV – the company with the doggie and the phonograph.

I arrived at my first session in Sloane Square to meet a lovely lad called Alan Best who, after the briefest of briefs, ushered me into a sound booth. I was hired for an hour.

"Okay Steve..." he screamed through the 'cans.' The red light came on and I proceeded. "The HMV Shop - more records - more tapes... more discounts." "Thanks, Steve, that's a wrap."

Somewhat stunned, I evacuated the booth and Alan presented me with an invoice I was to sign for £500. "That's it, mate. See you in three weeks." And so, three weeks later in the same booth, so the same red light flashed again.

"David Bowie," I said in my best Radio One voice! "Thanks Steve," yelled Alan.

And, a week later, plastered all over ITV and Channel 4 was the new HMV ad with old sexpot as the voice... “David Bowie. The HMV shop! More records, more tapes, more discounts!”

And, for the next eighteen months, I produced... “The Rolling Stones,” “Tina Turner,” “Elton John,” it went on and on. I wasn’t even a big star, I was just in the mix, but the money was there for the killing. Would it ever stop?

Of course not.

CHAPTER 30

Ooooh Look Who I've Met

One of the most enjoyable aspects of life as a TV music pundit was the time-honoured interview with the rich and famous popsters of the day.

In my case, another reason to meet those who were pinned to my bedroom wall all those years before.

As always it would all come down to 'likeability' and one's ability to put your interviewee at ease, ignore the camera and allow the conversation to flow.

"Okay – so as they say. Now, back to the show!"

Here now is a list of some of the most memorable interviews what I done in the 80s excluding Mr P Collins – and I'm leaving out the ones who were arseholes as I don't want to read this is in the top ten best-selling books from a prison cell.

My first ever TV interview? You can't get anything more frightening than Alice Cooper, arriving at the studio complete with whip and trademark snarl – and was a complete gent putting ME at ease!

Chatting with heartthrob, David Cassidy, in a Jacuzzi at a hotel in Mayfair. He invited me to join him in the water, so I did – and ended up drinking champagne till the camera ran out of film!

Entering a hotel suite to talk to Darryl Hall and John Oates, when Hall stands up and says, "Jeeze it's Steve Blacknell!" HA!

Playing table tennis with Bill Wyman whilst discussing his career with the world's top rock and roll band.

Nervously chatting to Gary Numan who was piloting his private aeroplane high up in the clouds.

Puffing and panting playing real tennis with Thomas Dolby. I nearly killed myself.

Talking to the always entertaining Motorhead guv'ner, Lemmy in LA. The interview was forty minutes long during which he consumed an entire bottle of Jack Daniels.

He once invited me for a drink, saying, "I'm on the wagon." When I arrived at the bar he was perched on a stool with a large vodka and a bottle of super strong white cider.

"Lem - I thought you said you'd stopped." Pointing at the table, "This isn't booze," he croaked – "It's fucking tea."

Nigel Planer, alias 'The Young One's' very own Neil, in a beaten down shack in Hammersmith, West London. I was drinking tea and the hairy hippy had spiked my drink with LSD.

There followed some incredibly trippy sequences that took three days to film, and were a total joy.

On the Breakfast Time sofa with the 'Morecambe and Wise of Rock & Roll' – Francis Rossi and dear Ricky Parfitt of Status Quo. Whilst reading the autocue, Rick put his foot in front of my mouth and I ended up doing the intro to them speaking into his shoe.

Tina Turner. I was, like so many others around the planet, totally enchanted with her. A few minutes into our chat, I just threw away the notes I'd nervously placed on my lap and we talked and talked. This was around the time when I was beginning to turn into a bit of a twit – and felt certain she fancied me.

I talked to her manager next day to see if she'd go out with me, and much to my chagrin he later called to say... no! WHAT a silly bugger I was – but I suppose if you don't ask you don't get.

Not so much an interview but a very brief chat with Mr Eric Clapton.

It had come to my notice that so many of my rock heroes had kids – and they'd all sit down on a Saturday morning and watch my Yoof TV show, '*Knock Your Block Off!*'

I was at a polo event organised by my new mate, Kenney Jones – he the man behind the drum kit of The Small Faces and latterly The Who. ANOTHER bedroom wall hero!

I was walking out of a big marquee tent when I noticed Clapton alongside me.

"Steve Blacknell – Knock your Block Off," I murmured.

"Eric Clapton – Cream," he replied, and with that we went our separate ways. A brief but unforgettable encounter with the guitar legend – or 'God' as he is sometimes known.

I was filming for MTV on a posh motor launch racing up the Thames with Mr Gary Glitter. He was in his heyday then, aptly dressed as a sea captain complete with cap and blazer. The champagne was flowing and we were being filmed from the top of Tower Bridge. We were alone, save for the driver, and in between slurps and takes he was rather tastelessly regaling me with his extensive sexual preferences and how he would f**k anything. Bearing in mind it was the mid-eighties when attitudes were more liberal, it was still pretty shocking stuff. To be honest, I didn't really believe him at the time and thought no more about it as he was such a loudmouth. Imagine my surprise and horror some years later when I discovered most of it was fact, not fiction. Looking back at his brashness and perverted sense of invincibility, it's amazing that he lasted all those years before he was found out.

Back in them 80s, I would put together charity events - as a Tommy Cooper fanatic I organised fundraisers where I'd invite a crowd of Cooper nuts, complete with their mandatory Fez, to meet in a club or whatever and tell their favourite TC gag to the assembled and do the Cooper laugh.

We were at the infamous (sadly no more) Mortons club in Berkeley Square. Houdini-like, the year escapes me, but it was around '85 I think. About seventy media/starry types assembled to raise money for the Nordoff Robbins Music Therapy charity. It was given further gravitas as it was hosted by fellow Cooper freak, Sir Anthony Hopkins - a well-known admirer of the great man who always delighted in donning said fez and going through a string of Cooper classics. With introductions over, he turned to me in character... "I'd like to invite Mr Steve Blacknell to come and tell a few of his favourite Cooperisms."

Up I stepped and nervously delivered my chosen gags.

"My wife stood by me for forty-two years - we only had one chair!" and "I was up in the attic with my wife the other day. Filthy and covered in cobwebs... but she's good with the kids," plus a few others and amidst uproarious applause stumbled off the stage, while Sir Anthony invited another to join him.

He may not have been on my bedroom wall, but I'll never forget that day.

As I've always said – "All our heroes have heroes."

And finally, there was Spike Milligan. I was interviewing him for a BBC show I did called *'Off the Record'* where I visited stars and talked about their record collection. Despite it being a 15-minute show, Spike insisted on five costume changes, and you can see us on YouTube walking down the road with him in his pyjamas.

I was later asking him about his favourite Beatles songs. "What about yesterday? I asked.

"Well," he said, stifling that famous grin of his, "Yesterday it was raining!"

Just like Cooper – because it was him it seemed extra, extra funny. The crew laughed so hard we had to stop for 15 minutes.

He was an extraordinary man in so many ways and I'll never, ever forget when the lovely Lynsey De Paul and I went for tea at his house... Spike just stared at me. "You remind me of me when I was young," he said.

Totally stunned I just murmured, "Thanks Spike." That was all I could say.

Spike Milligan may have been the funniest man who ever walked the Earth.

So, please do forgive the name dropping. I do HATE name dropping.

I was only saying to Paul McCartney the other day how much I loathe it.

CHAPTER 31

Birth of the VJ

By now, MTV was huge in the USA, and it had cut the need for artists to trek overseas.

I'd been approached by the knobs at EMI to take part in an experiment - a brand-new way of showing the visual side of music. Videos!

Back in the 60s, the Beatles had successfully used videos within the film *'Hard Day's Night'* of 1964 – which led many years later to MTV giving Beatles director, Richard Lester, an award for basically 'inventing' the music video. With its launch in NYC in August 1981, in one fell swoop MTV had revolutionised the music industry. Such a simple concept! Endless pop videos, linked by a team of video jockeys - now just simply known as VJs!

MTV was, in effect, 'wallpaper TV'. It was there in the background as a backdrop to everyday life.

Now and again, something would prick the ears, and the volume would be turned up - then down when the next one, not so appealing, played. It was 24-hour coverage and the phrase 'I Want my MTV' became such a household phrase that even the bigger bands were keen to push their big noses in, notably Dire Straits' 1985 U.S. number one, *'Money for Nothing'*.

And so, in the summer of '82, the late Capital Radio DJ, Mike Allen, and myself were chosen to helm the music video cable show - *Music Box* - where the music videos of the day would be linked by the VJ. They were exciting times, even though the show would be going out exclusively in the musical Mecca that is - Swindon!

EMI's very own Alan Parsons, he of The Alan Parsons Project, was given the task of directing the pilot. He had been the engineer on The Beatles' *'Abbey Road'*, *'Let it Be'* and Pink Floyds' *'Dark Side of the Moon'*, so he knew a bit about the music business. It was history in the making and I was presented with my very own 'Europe's First VJ' T-Shirt.

As the project gained pace, so it was farmed out to Europe and following its success, I received a call from one of the bosses at PMI (Picture Music International) which was now the visual arm of EMI. It was a whole division dedicated to making and marketing videos of the home acts, and beyond.

This particular *beyond* turned out to be a far-flung idea to pitch to MTV, U.S.A, a show that would feature all the happenings in the UK. The American charts were full of UK acts anyway – so it had a modicum of sense about it. Intrigued? Not arf!

So, I met with PMI top gun, Allasonne Lewis. She seemed quite ferocious on first impression, but as we talked over coffee, I could feel a sense of oneness and minds on the same track.

In much the same way that MTV had penetrated middle America and taken the latest 80s hits to a music starved populace, so we would show the same audience and more across the nation what was new and happening.

Although the States had given us so much culturally, don't forget that at various times through music history, the good old U.S. of A. had been a few steps behind the little old United Kingdom.

The Cars, a fairly innocuous rock outfit from Boston, were termed 'punk' there. They were a long way from The Sex Pistols, The Damned or The Slits. THAT was punk! They were AOR (Adult Orientated Rock or Any Old Rubbish) at most!

Platform boots had just hit Middle America. For a country so advanced in so many cultural areas; music and fashion were several light years behind us in Blighty!

It was decided that we'd shoot a 'pilot' for the yanks. Once more, Mr Parsons, temporarily defected from The Project to assume helm position. Allasonne would produce, and old big nose here would front the bugger. I was thrilled beyond words, me, a star in America? Shirley Knott!

At the time, I shared an agent with my old chum, John Altman, from EastEnders. She was the celebrated celebrity agent, Sharon Hamper, and we became thick as proverbial thieves. Long nights were spent clubbing, pubbing and rubbing shoulders with fellow 'personalities'.

Allasonne and I had become great friends and grappled with what the show could be called? After a few cocktails, one sunny eve, we fell upon the old war cry *'London Calling'*.

Well, that said it all really, it was London reaching out to the U.S.A. to tell of all that was new and funky in London town! So, that was it!

"Get your agent on board, quick," Allasonne whispered loudly to me one day in the EMI cafe. Weird coming from her as she held the purse strings, but it was a great soft shout that would get the pound notes a rolling in.

The next day, I visited Sharon at her Fulham flat. After explaining that it was to be an hour-long transmittable pilot, with me all over it like a nettle rash, she became rather motivated.

"How much do you think they'll offer?" she said.

"Well, I was thinking maybe two hundred and fifty a show," I ventured, not having a clue but staring blankly at a pool of money in my head.

"I'll ask for ten thousand a show," spat the Hamper. "EXSQUEEZE ME... Ten K??" spat I.

"Well, we'll see, Mr B," she said with an agents smile.

After weeks of toing and froing, my new friend, Sharon, and Allasonne came to an agreement.

One late Friday morning, the phone sprung into life. It was the Hamper.

"It's a grand for the pilot, then if it's sold its 3k a show."

"You are bloody joking!!" I yelled. "'SHITTTTT." The pilot was duly shot at Peter Stringfellows newly opened nightclub, The Hippodrome, in Leicester Square.

This was pioneering stuff and it felt as we had something very, very special. The credits were genius and it all fell into place.

The pilot aired on MTV U.S.A. to surprisingly huge acclaim.

We were a hit! We were signed up for a further eleven episodes, and the Hamper received more roses than she could find pots for! On paper, I was an 80's millionaire and this rocketed me into another space. Allasonne was the brains behind it, it was she who mainly picked up on shiny new talent. She had the magic touch.

"What do you think, Blacknell?" Was the regular question as she'd slide video number 47 into the player for review, or a rant, about a new band demo. And even if I hated it, it generally made the show.

I loathed Simply Red, but she loved their debut single, *'Money Too Tight to Mention'*. I hated it. She said, "The Yanks will love this."

We ended up filming their debut video in a snooker hall in East London, and that was the start of Mick Hucknall in the U.S. of A.!

Other transatlantic first glimpses included Marillion and Tracey Ullman to name but two! The big stars were queuing up to be part of the show. Duran Duran, Queen, Tina Turner, they all wanted to be seen by the ever-increasing millions of Americans who tuned in each month.

Our stage was London itself, but we always asked the stars where they wanted to be interviewed. This appealed to their ego and worked a treat.

With a crew of eight, and a 28k budget per show, this was real TV. We were blessed with an amazing director in Nigel Cole, a magician of light and sound who would go on to light up the big screen with 'Calendar Girls'.

We never really got on, but I so admired his array of skills behind the camera, and in the edit he was a marvel who could create magic with a solitary film camera.

As for yours truly, I had that solitary shoot day once a month. It was frenetic to say the least, leaping about London at 100mph and talking at the same pace! Everyone assumed I was on the marching powder, but to my credit, I never ever took even half a bitter before going on camera.

The show itself proved to be a massive success, attracting twenty-three million viewers and winning the coveted 'Ace' award for Best Music show.

However, after eighteen shows, I'd had enough! The money was rolling in in torrents but I felt we'd run out of steam. The figures were still fantastic, but I was urgently keen to move on.

I delivered my news to the PMI bosses one bright July morning, only to be met by the news that MTV were actually cutting back, and we were one of the first to go! But I was now stinko rich. Did I give a shit?

Although I was one of the business' 'nice guys', I was gradually turning into a bit of a self-obsessed knobhead, and, though my intentions to the ladies in my life were always good, I was not coping very well.

Life was amazing. The money was pouring in, literally like water.

Unfortunately, mine was slipping out through my hands each and every day. I was spending it like it was about to be made illegal. It was sheer unadulterated opulence.

I later joined Music Box Europe. Amongst our number were Timmy Mallet, Gaz Top, as he was known then, real name Gareth Jones – a Welsh TV presenter, and Amanda Reddington. We were a zany bunch indeed. Wacky and zany!

One bright spark had the idea we should record a single for our fans across the sea... which we did, complete with a hugely annoying video consisting of us being both wacky and zany! We were rather unfortunately called The Rat Pack too... the song was dreadful. *'Back To The Rhythm'* was a corny rap number that oozed yuk, but we became stars in Holland where it waddled to the dizzy heights of number 14 in the Dutch charts. Fame at last!

My own show was called 'Off the Wall'.

"If you want the stories, I've got 'em all, coz I'm Steve Blacknell and I'm OFF THE WALL!" I looked and behaved like the coke freak I really was, head butting the camera and shouting at passers-by in the street.

The Music Box boss, Julian Aston, was my director and we'd plough through the streets of London with Herbert here talking so fast none of us could really understand what I was on about.

My catch phrase was "I can exclusively reveal that..." and then deliver the pop news of the day. In fact, we'd pin the days' newspaper headlines to a clipboard, and I'd just read them off. We figured nobody in Germany would A. know any different, or B. give two hoots.

I was still functioning out there in 'medya' land! As the chap who put the 'a' into arse, I was flitting from club to club, hotel to hotel – the bigger and brasher, the fucking better.

With my regular acupuncture in the wilds of Cambridgeshire, I always went First Class. I recall someone asking why.

Why? "Because I can," I retorted.

Throughout those early 80s, I'd established a name with the youth of the day in the UK, but not many other places except the USA, where I continued to be big news.

I'd sit with Michael, my cigar-choking accountant in posh restaurants, he'd always pay, and concoct companies – designed for goodness knows what, giving them something wacky as a name – just because I could!

Hence the birth of Grey & Pink Ltd. named after my fave Caravan album in March '83 with its subsequent demise three years later at a lunch in the same eatery – with not an ounce of business done, and money cobwebs everywhere. Total cost £1800. Piddle. I had not a worry in the world.

CHAPTER 32

A DJ at My Own Convenience

I was still doing well telly wise. The odd pop up on an obscure prime time TV show where nobody really knew me at all, to BBC's Pirate Radio 4 hosting a three-hour daily show for kids and the odd segment on MTV USA.

Back in my plugging daze, I had, of course, become great pals with several of the DJs and kept in regular touch. One such was a true 'one off' - Paul Holmes. Although he'd accomplished a fair amount of notoriety in his native New Zealand, he had sought pastures anew and had made the decision to try it big in the UK. He ended up in the coveted 'drive' slot on Swansea Sound Radio. His irreverent style and tendencies to shout at his callers made him stick out like a sore leek and he was soon the talk of Wales! He and I became great chums and he was forever wrecked on my Chrysalis Records expenses.

Back in '77 and when I took girls down with me for a free weekend, he was the first to get 'stuck in' as it were. A real ladies man. Any record I played him on a drunken weekend would weirdly end up as a 'Record of The Week' a few days following. But that was the game. It was a people business

By the turn of 1987, Paul had had enough, maybe because of his rowdy and sometimes inexplicable behaviour. The mainstream had passed him by. Disillusioned, he decided to go home and try again. In the March of that year, he took over the breakfast slot on 1ZB, one of the nation's top stations.

It was a few weeks later when the phone pinged and there he was, Holmes himself. "Steve, me old beauty. Fancy a gig?" So it was that I became the 1ZB London Correspondent. What a gig! All I had to do was to rove around London, finding all the top spots and tourist havens and go live every Wednesday. It was 6.30am in Auckland - 7.30pm my time.

My debut on New Zealand radio did not turn out as planned. I was due to do a live piece outside Buckingham Palace. Although mobile phones were quite new, I was already equipped with the oversized talking brick that I pinned to my ear 24/7. However, that afternoon the previous night's excesses had proved too much for Mr Tummy and I was pinned to the toilet seat for hours with the dreaded shits. So, there I sat.

When the call came in at 7.30pm, Paul's show was just getting going and, as I heard my intro, I knew I had no choice but to go on.

"So, Steve Blacknell" Holmes bellowed. "Where are you today in jolly old London?" Straining every muscle south of my navel and doubled in pain, I replied, "Yes, Hi Paul... well today I'm right outside Buckingham Palace and... yes... yes... the flag is flying above the palace, that means Her Majesty is at home... and, hang on... I'm sure she can see me Paul, she's waving, she's waving!!!" as yet another deafening fart and splattering noises muttered from below. And so, the ten minutes went by as I stoically kept the chat alive.

"And next week, Steve... where will you be?" Paul gabbled. "Well, I'll be visiting Tower Bridge, Paul, and telling you some amazing facts about the crown jewels."

I later told him the situation I'd been in and being Holmes, he loved it.

From then on, for four months, I would do my report every Wednesday evening from my loo in Holland Park, often pulling the chain for extra effect. I always said that I was calling at my own convenience just to make him laugh live on air.

Paul did amazingly well, becoming the top daytime pin-up in New Zealand and, eventually, being knighted by the Governor General of NZ in 2013. Paul died a few weeks later of heart and cancer problems. SOOO sad.

CHAPTER 33

Coming Clean on Bulimia
1983

After finally conquering my Bulimia in 1982 via my new addiction, acupuncture, I had become 'clean' for the very first time in years.

I had not quite figured out how to talk about the emotional mountain I had climbed, but it came to me one day that to talk live on the TV might be the way to achieve maximum impact and reach as many sufferers as I could in one fell swoop. The powers-that-be had decided to give the divinely sumptuous, Ms Suzanne Dando, and myself our own slot within the show, wittily entitled 'I'm Blacknell - She's Dando'.

As a former gymnast, she was perfect to talk about addiction, in this case to exercise, which had become something of a 'thing' with the rise of gym membership and the Jane Fonda phenomenon. So, it was on a fine summer's day in '83, that I let on to a few million people about my little journey around some of the UK's finest bog-bowls. We were inundated with calls – one of which came from my Mum! "Well done," she said, "We always knew something had been wrong, but never quite knew exactly what."

I realised to my horror that, although I had confided to various friends of my problems through those six long years, in the heat of it all, I had forgotten to tell my parents. But they were coolness itself, and just let me know they were happy I was okay. I was overwhelmed. I think it's called unconditional love.

I had now taken to wearing even vaster amounts of mascara and foundation. I'd get a bit of stick but I didn't give a crap, and the more people poked at me, the heavier I slapped it on. I'll never understand how I managed to appear on Auntie Beeb looking as I did, but it has to be said, it was my outrageous look and demeanour that kept me away from the delights of prime time. A certain Mr Jonathon Ross would later get it right with his suits and lacquered hair. In one of his very first press articles a few years later, he stated that he ‘didn’t want to become another Steve Blacknell’. Well – he didn’t. But he did do rather well!

CHAPTER 34

Steve Who?

1985

By the spring of 1985, I had jettisoned most of my old chums – my darling Maggie who'd been so close, was a stranger to me and it was all my doing!

After parting company with Ms Hamper, I had a new manager called Deke Arlon.

He was already a legend 'back in the day' as a pop star of sorts but had carved a remarkable niche in artist management, steering the likes of Elaine Page, Sheena Easton, and Dennis Waterman to lofty heights! As a 'rising talent' I joined the clan along with a certain Captain Sensible, the beret-topped, madcap bassist with The Damned – who'd had a fluke number one with a version of '*Happy Talk*' that was so straight it was almost perverse. We would drink and talk crazy ideas, the most noteworthy being Sensible Foods, the world's first frozen vegetarian foods! Back in 1985 it seemed crazy – now, it doesn't.

Deke majestically underlined the theory that a successful manager or agent did indeed have the power to break an artist. All it came down to was how you stood in the pecking order! It sounded great to say you'd just joined Sheena Easton's fold but reality ranch was that someone like me was a 'C' list, 'on the up' type of talent, but was way, way down the pecking order. People like Deke would spend most of the day saying no to people after his top stars – while folk like me waited for the phone to ring. I'd later experience the same ethic in Tinseltown. So, it was my job to remind the boss that I existed.

Once a month or two I'd dare to call the office and ask to see him. It would get to the point where I'd forget who was working for who!

Typically, one day, I had made the call and was summoned to Deke's office for the precious meet. "Ah - Steve my boy, how have you been?" He said, "What can I do for you?"

"Well, I rather fancied doing a quiz show or something," I rambled.

As I finished my sentence, he was on the phone. "Get me Vernon at Yorkshire TV..."

Vernon Lawrence was the head honcho there and Deke had known him forever. "Yes, Vern. I've got the new Bruce Forsyth for you; he's right here with me. Yes... okay... that's great. See you soon." The phone clunked down. "Okay, you're on *'Through the Keyhole'* with Willie Rushton and Anna Raeburn week after next. Travel and hotel's paid for. £500 a show. Two shows. That okay?"

This was the show where David Frost would question three 'celebs' on a panel following a short film made by his co-conspirator, Lloyd Grossman, who would walk through a famous person's house, picking up items to 'hint' at the celebrity the panel had to identify. His Boston drawl was a strange diversion but he was perfect for the format and the show was a hit! Every time the panel made a wild guess, the audience would chuckle with mirth, in on the secret of the celebrity who huddled behind a screen only seen by the audience.

"Erm yes, Deke," I muttered. "Thanks, and see you again soon." I virtually bowed as I backed off out of the office. But no mistaking it, Deke was a real gent and one of the very best. And so it went. I did the shows, job done. I'd reminded Deke I existed.

The problem was that I was a pop music man, the wacky movie reviewer, so, when I went on those prime time shows, it was the wrong demographic,

"Ladies and gents, please give a big Keyhole welcome to Mr Willie Rushton," cooed the host, David Frost. Huge applause!

"To the lovely Anna Raeburn!" Hoots of hoorahs from audience.

"And, finally, our favourite pop pundit, it's Steeeeve Blacknell."

You could almost FEEL the audience turning to each other. Who the fuck is he? as I walked on to a polite pattering of palms.

But I had to play the game in more ways than one. They had a run through, so we knew how it all went. Then out would resonate the incredibly nasal tones of Lloyd Grossman. I often wondered if he actually knew who the 'celebrities' were. I can tell you for a fact he had no clue who I was, as nobody else there knew either.

So, they'd play his piece to camera as he walked through a celeb's house, picking out objects to offer subtle clues to lead the panel to guess whose house it was.

"Sooo, whoooo do you think would live in a house like this? Over to yoooo David."

A film reel came up for us to watch and I immediately recognized a familiar front door with its floral curtains. I played along and put forward a few questions, then I muttered to Willie and Anna, "It's Spike Milligan." They prodded me to offer the answer and everyone was amazed how easy it had been. I'd been there only two days earlier.

Now, the first reel round began.

There was a keyboard room, a cape slung over a chair and very familiar album covers on the wall. There was fashion magazines splattered across the lounge table and a glitter dress on the bed. I couldn't think for the life of me who it could be. The other two were clearly even less inspired - after all, I was the big pop pundit! After several infantile guesses we all gave up.

"Ladies and gentlemen," squealed Frost. "Please welcome the one - the only - Mr Rick Wakeman!!"

Willie had no idea who he was and shrugged. Anna 'looked' as if she knew him. Then there was me. I'd not only known Rick for many years, but I knew his then Mrs, as I'd promoted Blonde on Blonde – the pop duo of Nina Carter, his wife, and Jilly Johnson back in them there seventies.

Resplendent with his trademark long blond hair, on walked Rick, smiled to the audience and with his back to camera, glared at me and mouthed something very rude indeed.

Sadly, these isolated rare appearances on 'real' telly did zero to up my profile, and although still ankle deep in moolah, I would continue to define the 'B' list celebrity.

This was, in theory, a strange way of climbing the ladder, but in truth it really didn't work. I'd appeared on '*Celebrity Squares'* a year earlier but that had had nil effect on my road to TV stardom as nobody, including the wacky host, Lennie Bennett, had a fucking clue who I was.

I'd only got on the show as a well-known chappie, one of the show's exec producers, was after my botty!

The same thing happened with impressionist, Bobby Davro, who was enjoying prime time success on his Saturday night ITV shows. Another 'he who shall be nameless' TV exec I'd met at a posh party in Chelsea - who 'rowed for the other side' was angling for an 'alliance' and convinced the show's producers that Bobby should have a go at doing an impression of me. I'd been told to watch the show as I'd be surprised and delighted by his take on Mr B. Nothing like me whatsoever!! He had a mullet wig, a silver chain slung around his neck, an open shirt with matching chest hair and full-blown cockney accent!

Of course, whilst chatting to the lovely Davro several years later, I discovered that he too had no fucking clue who I was and had just seen a few video clips!

Totally crackers, and indeed those shows did me more harm than good!

So, it seemed best to do what I did best – jumping around in front of camera and talking at a hundred miles an hour!

CHAPTER 35

Knocking One's Block Off

1986-7

Whatever they might say about talent, there's one thing that gets you on in life more than ability. It's LIKE-ability! No matter how good you are at the given task – if you are a pain in the arse – well, who wants to work with that? There are ten people up for a gig – all with a shiny never-ending CV and all more than capable of doing the job in question. But who's going to get the job? Well, it will be he or she who emits like-ability and the vibe that they are not going to cause you problems. It's said that you can tell if you are going to like someone within ten seconds of meeting them. It's a bit like that indeterminable feeling when two pairs of eyes lock. You know they are the person for you.

I may have been many things with stupid addictions and more faults than the San Andreas Valley but, I've always been good with people, and people generally liked me.

I just can't help it!

And so it was, in my 80s TV career folk always knew that I wouldn't be a pain. I'd turn up on time, learn my lines, muck in with the crew, be nice to the autocue person and have a good laugh at the inevitable post show piss up.

Going back to *Knock your Block Off,* mentioned earlier, I got the gig following a call, in late November of 86, from a mate at Central TV in Birmingham. I was now handling my own business – so no more handing over twenty-five per cent commission, thanks very bleedin much!

It was a children's game show based on a Brazilian adult format – not the subtlest but certainly the most exciting I'd seen in years. There were two walls made from coloured cardboard bricks, two teams of tiny kids from schools around the country wearing helmets and equipped with 'bodging' poles.

The host would ask questions in machine gun fashion – and according to who got them right, bricks were bodged and prizes were won. There was also the addition of the infamous 'bean bag attack' where the kids would attempt to short cut the frenetic proceedings and topple the opponents wall with said bean bags! Speedy stuff – and it called upon someone who could treat kids like people and maintain the pace while running the game and a bawling, screaming crowd of mini-adults!

I was up against some much more familiar names, most of which have escaped in time, but surprisingly sailed through the audition.

I warmed immediately to the production team at Central TV. They were, in effect, the *Muppets* production team, from producer down to tea boy and all as camp as a tent park.

One by one, we all ran through the mechanics of the game – which looked easy on screen – but were in actuality a bugger to do at 100mph.

And so, I was to be in sunny Birmingham for two and half months recording the dozen or so shows. They were, in fact, a segment in a rather awful Saturday ITV mish mash show called *TX*.

I say with some pride that KYBO did shine amongst the mists of crap TV of the day – and as I've mentioned became a cult show with kids and their parents! The prizes were huge for 8-10-year-old kids - TVs, PCs and the like, and the competition was fierce. It was a total joy to do, and I loved each and every minute of it.

Backstage, things were a little less innocent! Each few days I'd do a voice over that would appear as if we looked at the prizes on offer! It was always a camp and corny phrase, but the team always wanted to push it a bit. The little bastards will never know, etc.

Hence much tittering on a Saturday morning when you'd hear me talk over the prizes of the day. "Make sure your balls go over the net – with this table tennis set!" Have to say, each day was a total experience.

There was a big round clock-type thing with different coloured segments, and when a competitor got a question right from me, they'd shout a colour and then I'd spin the clock to see what colour it landed on. One day during a break, I noticed a man behind the clock fiddling around and then it dawned on me - he was stopping it on order from the gallery to make the game run smoothly. Not in a kids show surely, but oh yes!

Far, far worse was to come. I'd always been known as a bit of a motor mouth on screen. And although I'd taken mountains of coke and speed, the one rule I had was never, ever when working.

Back in Birmingham all was going well. I was hanging about with the likes of Michael Elphick and Gary Holton in the Central bar – it was heaven with all the overly-camp team to laugh and drink with.

There was a knock on my hotel door one late Monday night. I was in bed after spending all day jumping around like a twat in front of screaming kids and a crew hell-bent on reaching the bar at 6pm.

"Steve? Hello," came a creaky voice. Opening up the door, I was confronted by Colin, the bloke in charge of production/fees etc. - the boring bits.

"What's up?" I offered, glancing at the clock. "We... er... we know you er... well, you have to talk a lot during this show," he muttered. "And we thought you - you know, may want something to sort of – erm - to keep you going."

"Coke??" I shouted.

"Why, yes, Steve. It's just to top you up, that's all."

Unbelievable – I'd been straight as a vicar's willy for weeks in this series as I knew that I had to be at the Blacknell best. So, now I'm offered it to keep me going! Damn cheek!

Tempted though I was, I politely refused the package and bade him goodnight. Tucked up in my bed, I lay and mused on the ridiculousness of it all.

The series came and went, leaving me with minor cult status amidst the junior population and their parents, a wedge of money, and not much of a voice left!

CHAPTER 36

Amen To That!

It was a blustery October evening as my recently acquired chauffeur, Ken, dropped the remains of me outside a rustic looking wine bar in the super trendy Mount Street. I was meeting a lady acquaintance, Julie was her name, an effortlessly trim beauty I had been seeing from time to time.

As we sipped Pimm's and ran over the antics of the week, my eyes felt drawn to the bar. There, a pair of deep blue Asian pupils were staring back at me. Drawing me in. As I glanced to her left, I espied the slightly Texan cowboy looking figure of a man. With my curiosity piqued, I steered Julie over to them and said a faint hello.

"I know you," said the Asian lady. "Steve, right?" It transpired that she was married to the cowboy bloke, and they lived in LA. She had been a fan of my *'London Calling'* show. "This is Alan," she beamed.

Now recoiling from the shock of such an unlikely fan in such an unlikely place, I shook his very big hand and was again caught in that instant state of familiarity.

I was suddenly back, standing in front of my bedroom wall in Dartford, staring at my Amen Corner poster.

"I'm Steve," I said, "Are you Welsh?"

"I am," he replied.

"Do you play the saxophone?"

"I do," came the reply.

"Are you Alan Jones from Amen Corner?"

"I am," he beamed.

I was staggered, stunned. Another bedroom hero had come to life.

We all talked, drank, and drank some more and chatted about life in Hollywood - how they just 'lurved' the British accent - and how maybe, just maybe, I might stand a chance out there.

It was indeed all too much. Cards were exchanged, promises made, and, as Julie and I strode off into the night, I kept smiling to myself.

About a week later as the sun set once again on Holland Park, the phone sprang to life.

"Hi... it's Trish... I've been thinking, could we meet?"

And we did, in the same bar where we had met. The idea? Blacknell takes Hollywood.

A brand spanking new pack of seeds were about to be sown. I wondered if this time they might produce something a bit more positive.

As I gazed over the tennis courts through my bedroom window, my mind was in a flurry. I turned to a flaked out Sooty.

"Well Soot," I whispered, "Maybe I should give it a go?"

CHAPTER 37

Sinus Sinus – For Fuck's Sake Sinus!

1987

I was finally getting a little bored of the 'kids TV' tag. Getting assaulted by Rod Hull's Emu at 4.30pm on a Wednesday afternoon children's TV show was not exactly my life's ambition, but it was still paying ze bills! But that was it. No more, enough.

My old producer chum and sometime drinking partner, Trevor McCallum, called me one lazy day in the late summer of '86 with a great idea for the '*Crackerjack*' slot of BBC1. "It's a grand a show – thirteen shows," he said. "I'm in," I shouted – I LOVE these kid's shows Trev!"

Rehearsals started in the Feb of 1987 at the BBC in Manchester. It was a sketch show with me the host, with long mulleted red hair, an obnoxious multi-patterned fake Hawaiian shirt, and a big leather belt with my trusted Sooty hanging off it.

I was, in truth, a sight to make your eyes sore. We had a studio full of screaming kids, the cast of actors doing okay sketches, and a guest band each week, all 80s popsters and with little in common with the screamers!

At 35, I was becoming a rather unpleasant pastiche of whatever it was I'd been four of five years earlier. I was descending into yukdom.

I had not been feeling well during the months of rehearsals. My head felt heavy and I had seething nasal pain. I'd seen a specialist and was informed that my sinuses were, to use a technical term, 'bolloxed'. Too much bowing to the lady in white had taken its toll and I was constantly dizzy and losing my balance. I was given some sweeties to calm the pain and it was resolved that I would have an op directly after I'd finished the series.

Suffice to say it was a painful experience... the searing hot studio taking its toll on the conk and surrounding areas – while I felt sick night and day. All this was not helped by a rather unhealthy addiction to the wholly dreadful *Neighbours* TV show. I would get a cab back to the hotel in lunch break just to watch the shit. On reflection, I must have looked more like a twat than I already felt.

The people were amazing but it's true to say that the legend that was *Crackerjack* was not under threat as it was treated badly by the press – and I came out of it worse than I went in. Relieved when it came to an end, I returned to London.

No sooner had my train touched down at Euston Station, I was straight into the private clinic to get me nose done!

The operation in question was the dreaded, pure evil that was the Caldwell Luc procedure.

AAAARGH!

Caldwell-Luc antrostomy is a pretty unpleasant operation to remove irreversibly damaged 'muckosa' of the sinus carried out when the condition couldn't be cured by medication.

It was a complete and utter bitch.

They were literally to take my top lip and peel it upward till the sinus's were exposed, then they simply drilled new ones!

Having had a few unnecessary ops, just because I could, I began looking forward to the whole process. Also, I felt in some ways that my time was done on the telly. I was still drowning in money – and maybe it was time for a rethink.

"Mr Blacknell," grumped the overweight, balding gent at the surgeon's office in Harley Street. "I'd just like to make you more than aware that this operation, though perfectly safe, can leave you scarred and bloated – so you will have to remain indoors without any contact with the outside world for up to three months. The risk of infection is just too great."

This all sounded incredibly dramatic and actually, a bit of a hoot! The other good bit about all this palaver was I was a rich kid and could actually choose what meds I could have. So, there I sat, one November morning of 1987 in a darkened room at the private hospital with a Dr. Evans, meticulously going through the options. Eventually we worked out a concoction that would send me into inner space prior to getting my gob cut open. It was heaven!

As I arrived back at the Holland Park flat, I was already excited over the fact that I was now literally on my own for twelve weeks – just Mr Blacknell and me, three months in complete and total isolation – no face-to-face contact whatsoever, and so it began. I was literally a prisoner in my own home.

Friends began dropping off food parcels at the door or by a rope dangling out of the flat window - I even did pieces to camera for Breakfast TV with a smuggled radio mike.

I was alone, no people, no drugs, no booze - nothing. It felt very, very weird. My face was swollen like a giant ostrich egg and blood red with throbbing pain. It was not very nice.

Each morning I'd take the bandages wrapped around my face and dispatch the plugs in my nose to the bin before I had to inhale salt water and expel gallons of mucus into the sink. God knows where it all came from.

I'd often get Tehidy Hospital flashbacks – but now the tables had truly turned.

My days were spent sprawling on my big round bed watching videos of my favourite TV shows and the occasional one of yours truly to remind me what the hell I did in life. Each night I had tuna spaghetti with clams. That was it, every night, the same. But I loved it. After a few weeks I began to feel a certain calmness had descended on my person. I felt good!

I was soon experiencing that lovely feeling of being excited about the next day and what it may bring.

Trish was staying in town for a few months so she'd knock and leave ridiculous first aid packages for me, but NO booze, NO drugs. I felt amazing!

My face now had more colours than Joseph's sodding overcoat – it was a total mess. But bit by bit, day by day, it settled down and it was becoming clear that it was decision time. It's said that clarity is achieved by a lack of alcohol – and I think that in my Holland Park flat, over those weeks, I began to see 'the light'.

The thoughts I'd been having pre-op now turned into post-op reality as I pondered my future. What next; yet another kids show… at my age? Another anonymous game show? Or an appearance on yet another bloody 'pop' show?

Gradually the whole thing began to assemble in my somewhat fresher brain.

A challenge! I needed a new challenge. It all seemed clear. I had an audience in America thanks to *London Calling.* Should I, could I, give Hollywood a shot?

I had met Cindy, a voluptuously paper-thin brunette fashion model at Tramp. She was a tall stunner with legs that finished just under her earlobes, and we reconnected talking on the phone during my incarceration. I was beginning to feel a bit frisky. We set a date for dinner at mine once my isolation came to an end.

With the 'all clear' from the clinic and now allowed to drink myself stupid if I wanted, we took up shagging with a vengeance.

So, here I was, still richer than I needed to be, fashionable girl in tow, and back out on the town. But it all felt pretty shallow, and I still needed to make a decision on my future. In a vague attempt to return to my spiritual self I took another week off and just stayed at home and fasted and drank lakes of water.

It was the Friday of that week that I made my play! Sitting cross-legged on my lounge wooden floor I tinkered with a fifty-pee coin. 'Heads its Hollywood, tails its Holland Park' went through my head as I tossed it into the air. The coin loitered in 2001 airspace as my world made ready for whatever it determined to be the right path. As it plonked onto the floor, I suddenly became aware that Paul Young's *'Everything Must Change'* was playing on the radio. Heads for home, tails for Tinseltown.

Tails. Change it was. Hollywood beckoned.

I informed Trish at her hotel that my mind was made up!! True stardom awaited me. This was going to be a breeze! What a stonking adventure!

An old gag popped into my refurbished headspace...

"You should go to Hollywood – the walk will do you good."

But I wondered – Did I really have what it took to conquer Tinseltown?

Well, only one way to find out.

Do it!

CHAPTER 38

One Yank and I'm Off

So, enraptured with the move, I left my flat exactly as it was, in the hands of the lovely Cindy and my beloved sister. I had a semblance of a goodbye party where I assembled all my female conquests, had a few drinks, packed my bags and naffed off!

It was only later that Maggie would tell me how absolutely crazy that was. It was like an exercise in pure ego drizzled with more ego!

But Trish, the manager, was now in command and all I had to do was to follow orders!

I had quickly gathered as many validations as I could from my BBC colleagues, and anyone I'd ever shared a studio, bar or bed with. All these were to get me the notorious H1 certificate. The bit of paper that would let me work in the USA – which would eventually lead to getting the holy grail of the Green Card – that meant I was officially American too.

As I was soon to discover, the one thing to know about Hollywood is that, no matter who've you've met, whatever you've done when you tread those first daunting steps on to the LAX tarmac, you enter a very different world.

Tinseltown itself is another planet – and for those who take the transatlantic plunge, it's an excursion into a dehumanised roulette wheel – a lion's den of false smiles, and false hopes. But the great thing about the town is that they give everybody a break! You may as well tear up that phoney CV or even the real one that you've slaved away on for months before.

Mass murderers, Ku Klux Clan members, arsonists – even drummers! The doors were always open!

"I've enjoyed reading your resume, Mr Blacknell."

"Why, thanks – I enjoyed making it up!"

Mine was bulging with references from the BBC, Channel 4 – even Buckingham Palace. Due to my Duke of Edinburgh Award activities I'd gone from Bronze to Gold and was as proud as one could be. But as I was to learn, oh so quickly, that all meant nothing.

Meanwhile my wonderfully supportive family were once more saying bye-bye. Bless them forever for their love and support.

So, as I touched down at LAX that stinking steamy day on Jan 4th 1989 – my bones were throbbing with anticipation and my brain with trepidation.

Could I REALLY do this?

I was met by a beaming Trish in her oversized jeep – and as we sped towards the Hills, I could see the legendary Hollywood sign. The dream maker, the dream killer!

I was to live with her and Alan the Sax Man. They both lived in a lovely little house on the corner of North Stanley in groovy West Hollywood. It was a buzzy neighbourhood with funky tree lined streets and it just smelled of opportunity.

A far cry from downtown Kent and the orange bedroom wall.

Trish owned a clothes store on the super trendy Melrose Avenue and Alan was managing a spikey, garish would-be Guns 'N' Roses-ish outfit called the LA Guns. I was so excited I could hardly poo.

The drinks flowed, plans were made and one drunken night Trish and I formed 'A Yank and a Brit Productions.' But was the world ready for it!! Well, we thought it was.

As the shock of it all wore off in a few days, I suddenly thought, 'Fuck it - my flat'.

I'd left it in a dreadful state in the dainty but unlikely hands of sexy Cindy. She was going to stay there for a while and I'd settle the mortgage etc. from LA. Looking back, it shows what a complete dumb schmuck I was. After a few weeks my sister let herself in to find it trashed and almost unrecognisable. Then, over the next months they found dry rot in the building and, as I ploughed on in Hollywood, my former London life, and my bank accounts were, literally, crumbling!

At night we'd plot the launch party of our new company, and what we'd wear at the Oscars. Only in Hollywood would these things seem possible! Every Friday night we'd stock up on crap blush wine and around midnight, Alan, would stumble to the spare room and produce his saxophone.

With Trish out of the way, we'd turn up the stereo, and the thumping tones of my favourite Amen Corner track, '*Bend Me Shape Me,*' would resonate down the avenue. I always imitated the band's singer, Andy Fairweather-Lowe, and we'd laugh till we pissed ourselves.

Little did I know that lovely Andy would also become another bedroom wall chum when I lent him my jacket to wear on the Roger Waters 'Wall' tour many years later.

Only in Hollywood could I be dancing through the night with one of my bedroom wall heroes – it felt like the place to do it!

After I'd been there for three short months, the Hollywood signs were looking good. I was signed to major agencies and being a Brit was a huge plus!

Trish was working a blinder getting my size 11 feet through the doors. And once I got in front of the big boys, I worked my Cockinese charm to huge effect.

I was now signed to the William Morris Agency and The Gersh Agency

The latter had been formed back in 1949 and was always seething with huge household names. My interview had been short, sweet and, to be honest, a dream. The VP was a certain Peter Young and it was his stable I was to join.

They managed Danny Devito, Kathleen Turner and a certain man mountain and wrestler extraordinaire, Hulk Hogan. 'Hulk' or Terry Bollea to his family and friends, had already made a few movie appearances but was determined to be a star on the silver screen. Over drinks one evening at the infamous Barneys Beanery, Peter was in ebullient mood. "Let's get Hulk away – and you're next," he enthused. "Cheers!"

All I needed was that elusive break.

'Just get me in that door and I'll show you what I can do.' I was so full of confidence I was ready to explode!

CHAPTER 39

Being Jahhhhn Clllleeeess

I was getting known as the new John Cleese meets Robin Williams.

The Americans love that. They describe people as something 'meets' something. A blended character. It's called the 'Elevator Pitch' when in the time said elevator gets to your designated floor you've hit your helpless prey with a super swift pitch of your current project.

So, I was 'JAHHN CLEEESSS meets RAHBIN WILLIAMS' and take it or leave it moosh.

I didn't mind the comparisons one little bit. Indeed, JAHHN CLEEEESS was big news and 'A Fish Called Wanda' was terminally hip at the time, and as a big nosed Brit, the auditions were rolling in.

If you recall the Mel Brooks 'Blazing Saddles' scene when Hedley Lamarr, the main antagonist, is recruiting bad guys, there is a queue a mile long around the cowboy block.

"What do you do?" he questions a tall bearded man. "I rustle cattle."

"Next." The next ugly villain moves forward to answer the same question to which he answers "Rape - and Rape."

"You said rape twice."

"I like rape," replies the villain. Maybe, that line wouldn't play so well today but it's still a winner!

However, the line of would-be gang members include: white, black, midgets, Ku Klux Klan, all the varieties of humankind. That was what I was confronted with that scorching morning waiting to audition for a shampoo ad.

The line round the Burbank lot went half way to Malibu. Chinese, Lebanese, Cockinese, Africanese, Mexicans, amputees, tall ones, thin ones, fat ones, some as big as yer head! Humans of all shapes and sizes - but not one that I could see looked ANYTHING like JAHHN fucking CLEEES!

In Hollywood they call it a cattle call, where every agent in town, upon sniffing the silver dollar, tells everyone and their mother's hairdresser with a pulse to turn up just in case.

By now I was brimming with confidence, clear in the knowledge that, to the average Tinseltown person, I had a slice of roast beef in my top pocket and a picture of the Queen tattooed on my arse. I was the embodiment of all things Brit! There I stood in my best bib and tucker. Surely, I MUST have stood a chance. After waiting in the soaring heat for well over two hours, I was finally summoned into the casting area.

It being the earlier days of my Hollywood trail, I'd no real idea of the immense span between British and American humour. As in them yanks don't do 'irony'.

But I'd try!

On the casting form where it said SEX, I'd always put 'Not at the moment thank you'.

Once in the room, faced with the stoniest of faces, I'd always put on the accent a bit, especially in fun scenarios like this – where Brit was key. It sometimes worked but here I knew a Pythonesque approach might play well for me. "Next is Mr Steve Blacknell," thus spoke the casting assistant

"Come on in Steve," mumbled the faceless director, "Tell us a little about your background.

"Well," I began, as I turned my head to look behind me. "It's a white canvas with a black frame." Silence. Rock solid frozen silence. It had passed over their heads faster than Concorde itself… and… more silence."

But then…

"Did you hear that, Mike?"

"SAY THAT AGAIN. SAY THAT AGAIN!"

"It's a white…" Then a shout.

"It's JAHHN FUCKING CLEESS! JAHHN FUCKKING CLEESS, I TELL YOU."

And that would be the norm. Everywhere I went I was 'JAHHN FUCKING CLEESS!'

As it happened, the shampoo company were looking for a John Cleese 'type' for a huge network TV commercial. Big buckaroos! Having convinced them I was in fact Cleese but in a pair of shorts – I felt, maybe, the big moment had come! After all, how many Cleese-alikes could there be in town? I was a 'shoe-in' whatever the hell that meant.

At this point in time, the real Cleese was commanding about a million dollars per ad. So, obviously, the client was seeking the cheaper version - enough to satisfy the brand but not enough to break its bank!

So, I did my 'shtick' and headed home full of hope. After FIVE call-backs spanning all of three months, there I was in the final two for this life-changing commercial. At last, I stood a chance.

Again, I went through my 'schtick' and played the lines to the always stony-faced casting person.

Out on the lot I was thinking this could be it! A 50/50 chance of a network commercial. I went home that day brimming with certainty. I had always been in touch with Mum and Dad back home so, when I called them at home in Hampshire I was, as always, full of the Tinseltown spirit.

"This could be it!" I stuttered. It seemed a long way from '*Knock Your Block Off*'!

Three days later, Pearl from my agents William Morris, called. As she spoke, I was quivering with expectation.

"Well, Steve. I'm afraid you didn't get it," she said solemnly.

"Mind you – nor did any of the other guys."

"Pardon me," I enquired with a lump in my throat the size of a golf ball.

"Yes, they gave it to John Cleese!"

What a waste of time and brain tissue. But hey! Four months of hope for glory, and they went and hired the bloke they couldn't afford.

Who'd do a thing like that?

Well, if anyone would - Hollywood!

CHAPTER 40

Fire Down Below!

Having been brought up in Peckham in London and grown up in darkest South East Kent, I had as normal a life as is humanly possible. Drama in my hometown of Dartford was when the local record shop closed or the local football team reached the first round of the FA Cup. It was normality with a capital N. Life in the suburbs was pretty dull stuff.

It's no wonder then that as the home of the movie industry and all things crackers, Hollywood had its own share of drama. To put it mildly, things happen in Tinseltown that could never happen anywhere else. It's the place where everything and anything is possible. As I was to find out to my cost!

Ken Gold and I had been great chums since we met at Jive Records in 1981. He was already established as a respected songwriter. He had co-penned the Real Thing hits *'You To Me Are Everything'* and *'Can't Get by Without You'*. After the resounding success of the fictional Tight Fit and the somewhat dodgy but incredibly successful cover medleys such as *'Back to The 60s'*, there was an album to do – and Ken had been brought in to twiddle the knobs.

We had remained great pals with our own particular brand of humour, and when he decided to give LA a once-over, we decided to get an apartment together. We took to calling each other 'Babe'. God knows why but it stuck.

One fine summer's day, Trish invited us both to drinks on her friend's yacht that was moored in the ultra-cool Marina Del Ray, North America's largest man-made harbour and home to the rich and famous. We were very excited as both he and I saw this as the first beginnings of a brand-new adventure.

It was around 3pm when we clambered aboard and as the ripples danced upon the hull, we chatted excitedly about just how we'd take on all comers and be the talk of the town. I'd be the new JAHHHHHN CLLEEESSE etc. – and he, Britain's answer to Burt bloody Bacharach.

Sandy, the ebullient and overly tanned owner, produced an ice bucket rammed with beer and as the rings pulled so we beamed – it was going to be amazing.

"Cheers, guys," yelled Trish, a few yards away. "Here's to you and watch out Hollywood!"

"Cheers," we chimed. "HOLLYWOOD!"

We cast off as the first glug of Bud Light met the back of my throat. Having travelled only for a couple of minutes, I was suddenly aware of a rumbling beneath me. The deck started to shake, as did I, then a bright red and blue flame flew skywards past my eyes. Then… silence. I looked at Ken. He stared at me. His eyes suddenly widened.

"AAAAAGGGHHHHH," we screamed almost in unison. The pain - white hot pain, like a knife through the brain.

"What the fuck is it?" I felt my senses turn a burning red. I looked down and could not believe what I saw. My right leg was literally on fire. The smell of burnt flesh filled the air.

"What the hell, Ken??" I could see his shorts were charred - the pain was getting worse, I didn't know what to do.

"BABE, you okay?" he screamed. I had no idea, no sense of time or place. My head felt as if it were about to burst. I could just make out that my rubber shoe had melted onto my right foot making one sticky smouldering mess. Instinct literally kicked in and I stumbled to the side of the yacht and kicked my right leg in the air as hard as I could. My molten shoe flew into the air and plopped into the water. I looked down to see that half the skin on my foot was missing.

Everything stood still. The seconds passed like hours. Ken was shrieking, "MY COCK'S ON FIRE!"

Everything was passing in slow-motion. His shorts were blackened, he ripped them off and threw them overboard. Trish was screaming. Sandy was shouting at the top of his voice to neighbouring boats, "HELP! – WE'RE ON FIRE!"

It was bedlam. Sheer, total panic set in and all hell let loose. We were jumping like frogs on crack in total disbelief at what had happened. Trish was trying to calm us down as Sandy struggled to turn the boat around. We were only a hundred yards out but it seemed an ocean away from dock as he struggled to bring about the wallowing craft back to safety.

Minus eyebrows, we were now staring at each other, eyes like red-hot saucers. Ken's lower half was scorched and my poor foot akin to a faded Christmas candle. The pain was unreal. It was above hurt. It was as if the world had stopped and we were in limbo. We began to understand what had happened. A split in the engine had sent a jet of searing flame into the air and split us asunder like Moses parting the Red Sea.

When we finally hit the quayside, Sandy and Trish rushed to find a phone, as we wriggled and screamed and scrambled to get off. As luck / fate would have it, the infamous Cedar Sinai Hospital, complete with burns unit, was just fifteen miles away. An ambulance arrived in a matter of minutes – which felt like hours. We were whisked on board in a flash, and away we went, sirens blaring and pulses in Formula 1 mode as we sat covered in blankets blankly staring at each other.

It was so fortunate that it was only a half hour skedaddle up the 405 to Cedar, and before long we were in the emergency arrival ward, which was spookily empty for a Saturday afternoon. As we lay next to each other – it all began to really hit us - the popping of the beer can, the cheers, and that jet of fire that seemed to come from nowhere.

"I think me balls are okay, Babe," quipped the now vaguely coherent Ken. I was not so sure. I dared not look down.

"I'm not sure but it feels like my foot has fallen off," I spluttered.

We waited to be seen. After what, again, seemed like an eternity, a nurse hurried in to see us and took a brief look before exiting as quick as she had come. It felt as if my foot was being ironed. The pain was unbearable.

"Babe, we gotta get some pain relief, this is fucking nuts," muttered Ken.

There we lay, for nigh on an hour, screaming obscenities at the top of our voices. Every now and then a nurse would pop in and tell us that "Someone will be right along." But nobody came.

I was close to blacking out when a familiar figure appeared at the door. It was Trish.

"Hi you guys. It's okay, all sorted!" Sorted? The very next minute a team of three medics appeared with a vast array of syringes and plastic cups rattling with pills. From sweaty panic, we were in cuckoo land within minutes. "Thank God," I bellowed as they tailed out of the room.

It transpired that it was only when Trish had arrived and flashed her friendly American Express Card that we were allowed any pain relief. A grim reminder that how well and truly fucked the 'Land of Opportunity' is with its medical insurance system – and how very, very lucky we are in the UK to have that most precious of commodities, the NHS!

Babe had got off reasonably lightly, with a scalded right bollock and an eyebrow lift. Herbert here had caught it rather badly and I had sustained third degree burns on my right foot. I had been well and truly clobbered and I never let Ken forget how I'd taken the brunt of the devil's wrath – the lucky bugger!

I never saw Sandy, the tanned man, again. There was talk of compensation – but it never appeared.

After dropping Ken off, Trish and I headed for home. I was by now a floating, jabbering mess. I had enough morphine in me to keep Janis Joplin going for a month. My leg was bandaged from above the knee down to the base of what was left of my foot, my face beetroot red. Not exactly the image I'd hoped to hit Hollywood with.

Alan, the late-night saxophonist, was there to greet me. "What the shitting heck have you been up to, boyo? Let's have a drink!"

Trish didn't drink. But when Jonesy and I drank, we really fucking drank. He produced a bottle of my favourite tipple, the Jack of the Daniels. "Thats yours," he said. "Now tell me all."

It occurred to me at the time and indeed still does now, that when you're an addict – well – you're an addict, and you have to run with each and every aspect of the phenomena.

Now and then, my mind flashes back to various traumas I've been faced with over my life. ALL sad events warranted an excuse to drink! It was always okay to get really pissed up. The 'get out' clause haunts me to this very day. It doesn't drown grief and pain but it lets you be the addict you are.

I've been drunk quite a lot in my time on planet Earth – but that night – with the cock of the tail of morphine and the nectar of Lynchburg, Tennessee flowing through my veins – I was King of the Hill!

Trish had been, as usual, quite amazing. She'd taken me on to be a Tinseltown sensation. But now she was nursemaid to a hairless, charred Cockney.

And nursemaid she was. I was to be taken each and every morning to the Santa Monica hospital – down by the sea, there to be debrided, that's the removal of dead or infected tissue to allow regrowth. I could walk with the aid of a stick but I was assured things would get worse before they got better! It was pure unadulterated hell.

Until I hit America, I'd been a stout vegetarian, occasionally vegan if it suited the interview. But with my new diet regime, meat was the order of the day. Meat, meat and more meat. Red meat, as red as my face, and the redder the better.

It was good for skin regeneration. I was to eat beef three times a day before, during, and after meals, and if I could ram a sausage or meatball down me pudding chute in between, then good to go!

Appertaining to the tragic death of 'Friends' star, Matthew Perry, in 2023, yet another Tinseltown tragedy, I understand that at one stage he was taking fifty-five Vicodin tablets a day.

As part of my pain management, I was prescribed just four Vicodin every twenty-four hours and was pretty well off the case, so God knows what state he was in!

However, I knew that an opioid blocks the pain messages to the brain and was thrilled I could have them legally. I'd had a few now and then, washed down with a large Jack and Coke they worked a right treat, so I began to scoff copious amounts at every opportunity. I'd lie to Trish about the amount I was taking and often tell her I'd lost a pack so I could get some more.

Aside from the unmitigated damage it does to mind and body, a lesser drawback was that it glued your poo department. Total blockage! As in nothing, but nothing, was going to escape. No more parking your breakfast! This was serious shit, or, actually, everything but.

So, as the sun arose to once more bake the hills and the hopeful, every morning I'd neck a few pills with a glug of JD, and settle into my newly acquired wheelchair.

I was now officially a Californian cripple. A few months earlier, I was walking tall through the London streets with a fat wallet and even bigger ego!

Each morning, Trish would heave me into the jeep, drive down to Santa Monica to the local hospital, and dutifully wheel me in straight to floor twelve for hypnosis!

Once I'd pictured waterfalls and Sark in the Channel Islands, my favourite hideaway, and listen to crap *musak* through the earphones, I was carted off to floor three for the debridement.

I'd lie down on a stretcher and be unceremoniously hoisted aloft and across the room like an out-take from *'Young Frankenstein'* then lowered into a vat of steaming disinfected near-boiling water. There I'd lie for what felt like a lifetime until a big fat nurse would approach, tongs in hand.

I knew what was coming! Slowly, very slowly, she'd peel off my saturated bandages, and as she peeled, I could feel my third-degree skin go with it. The pain was indescribable. I would often pass out. I mean, I liked a bit of drama but this was ludicrous!

Now back in dry dock and with new bandages in place, it was back home for a beef brunch, a tot of Uncle Jack, more pills and more often than not futile attempts to talk business with Trish. And what was I doing there anyway?

I wanted my Mummy.

This cavorting, carefree man about town had now morphed into a burbling wheelchair bound piss-head, cavorting about the Hollywood streets in a red wheelchair with a bottle of Jack under my blanket. Not quite the impact I'd been keen to make.

And so it rolled on for four months. Even when the pain eventually faded, and my foot was healed, I still begged Trish for my beloved Vicodin. By now my arse and stomach had colluded to resemble a Buddha. So stuffed and bulbous were they that I could hardly move. But it was worth it. Day by day, though still as high as the proverbial kite, I began to make plans.

Meanwhile, poor Ken was still nursing his wedding tackle. That rather sensitive area had miraculously survived the flames, and he was bleeding lucky to have anything workable there at all. Neither of us had an eyebrow left.

We later discovered there had been a malfunction in the engine room on the boat, directly below us as we clinked our congratulatory beer. The resulting dragon's breath had nearly done for us. In fact, it was only later we realised we'd been hugging right over the flame's exit point, and God knows what would have happened if that had hit us in that moment. It didn't, and doesn't, bear thinking about.

The daily combination of hypnosis, pills, plus liberal snorts of Jack Daniels and endless steak and burgers soon became normality itself.

It would take just over five months of wheeling myself around Hollywood with the Jack strapped to my back before I could properly walk again. The $40,000 hospital bill would have been enough to put me back in A&E but, thankfully, a chum in the UK insurance business managed to fiddle the cross-Atlantic books and I emerged financially unscathed, save for a scar on my left ankle that's still there - a painful reminder of my somewhat inauspicious entry into the Hollywood showbiz scene.

Life there was not easy. Mixed with the whole abnormality of the place itself was the constant strain of the next audition added to by my UK funds being squandered on trying to save my flat – so there was an evergreen money famine. I was in new territory - bereft of funds and in a bit of a Branston Pickle.

I've always been a drinker, and a good British drinker at that. I knew when I'd had enough as I would fall over and be sick everywhere.

But drinking in Tinseltown was sort of frowned on, at least in public. It would be a sparkling water and a spot of minced bream for lunch, then a bottle of gin and three grams of coke in the evening. What a weird bunch!

So, now and again the pressures would get the better of me and I'd take a bus over to Burbank, Malibu, or even better, to the resort town of Santa Monica. I'd also carry a few cans of strong crap lager.

Now mercifully fully recovered and with all the pressures of 'making it' too much to bear, I would toddle off to the Santa Monica seaside.

One stinky hot day, my shoulder bag clunking with beer cans - swimming trunks at the ready, I was too.

There was something about the pancake culture of Hollywood, the smell of the city, those constant battles deep inside that refreshed a man and made you feel there was always hope. The sea, the rolling waves, the beach bikers, the golden sand, it was like a jab in your arse!

Finding my spot took little or no time at all... and so there I lay, classic rock radio in my ears and 99% shit lager pouring down my throat; Peace, away from the falsity and craziness of life in a pressure cooker. A quick movement, and in a flash my pants were off and my trunks on. Time for a paddle or maybe a dip. I'm actually afraid of deep water: I was pushed in a pool as a child and it still frightens the shit out of me, but as the sun blared down and the cheap beer started to hit me, it all came to me, this is the way to relax. It's all here. I'm living the dream!

As I waded into the blue Pacific, all my tensions seemed to disappear and, with a defiant grump, I lowered myself gently, until I was sitting on the sea bed, head just above water, this for me was a huge deal. The Young Man and the Sea. At last!

I turned to see...

'DANGER – RAW SEWAGE – DO NOT BATHE!' And sure enough, there, right behind me was a huge open rusty pipe gushing muck into the sea where I sat.

That was the end of my flights of fancy sea-wise. As I was a hypochondriac, I was convinced I'd die an unnatural, smelly death. So, no more day trips.

Whenever I enter a place that stinks, or there's a rotten smell in the air, you'll often hear me say, "Yep – that's just like sitting in sewage!" And when anyone says, "Well, you don't know what that's like."

I just say, "Yes, I do!"

CHAPTER 41

Hello Silver Lady

To get an agent in the UK is akin to finding a lottery ticket and winning the same night. The Brits are soooo anal. You have to have credentials a yard long that validates the sheer audacity of even thinking you're worthy of representation. Not so Hollywood.

It may be a crappy crepe of a town with the sincerity of Beelzebub, but as I keep saying, they do give you a break.

They never dismiss the idea of the new kid on the block making good. Just in case they can claim involvement in someone's success.

"Hey Barb - you know that Steve Black-Nell? Well, I always knew he'd make it. We go waaayyy back!"

The Hollywood insurance policy. Tried and tested.

There was an unwritten rule in Tinseltown. Give it three years, then, if sod all's happened, quit and head for home as you'll be knocking on the same doors all over again. Easier said than done.

The two Babes, Ken and I, were now happily settled in our two bedroomed place on Alta Vista Blvd, a quiet West Hollywood side street off Sunset, complete with swimming pool and all the amenities one would need to survive the rigours of life in this terminally bonkers and dangerous town.

There was a four-foot wide balcony where one could take in the somewhat obligatory view of the Hollywood sign, imperative for newcomers to the gold laden streets of Tinseltown itself.

Now burn free, we decided to have a big welcoming party. The great thing about life there was that the local community too gave you a break – as in a chance to show what you can or can't do – and folks turned out in droves to check anyone new in town. So, Ken, the tidy bearded Charlie Drake lookalike, and old big nose here seemed to kick up a lot of interest.

Thinking we may get a dozen or so show ups through the jungle telegraph, by 9PM the place was like an alcoholic Woodstock! There were agents and agents' friends, D-list celebs and D list celeb's friends... it was seething.

A good Brit presence too. I'd known Siobhan Fahey from the early Decca days when she was on reception. She had become a big star with Bananarama and she messed in with the hangers on, as did our old chum Alan Love, or 'Luvvy' as we knew him from his days on stage in *'Jesus Christ Superstar'* and *'Tommy'* – he too was seeking Stateside stardom!

My new chum Tobbe Hansson, a genial Swedish nut, was there with a bevy of beauties, and the floorboards rocked as Ken and I felt like we were in a dream. The dream that is Hollywood.

I'd met Tobbe at a movie screening in Westwood one balmy Friday night, and before long we started chatting about life back in the UK and English humour. He may have been Swedish but I was astounded to learn that we shared a hero in Tommy Cooper. He did the worst impression I'd ever heard but he was hysterical in every way. Within a few weeks we had become inseparable.

He was a photographer and musician. I spent many happy times in his apartment just shooting the shit and watching old Cooper VHSs, both of us laughing till we cried.

Ken and I had always shared a pretty bizarre comedic bond. When we said goodbye any time we'd have to say it around forty times as we backed off each other into the distance. "Alright Babe?" was the day-to-day remark. "You alright Babe?" "Yes... good. Are you alright, Babe?" and so on.

We were SO English!

There was a brilliant quote from the late, great English eccentric, Vivian Stanshall. When the *Bonzo Dog Doo Dah Band* – his crazed jazz spoof combo, a hugely weird looking bunch of ex-public-school musos who were trying their luck in the USA – they were stopped in Kansas one day by a burly town cop. "Say... how you guys doing? You're in weird territory out here boys. You're looking kinda weird... how you gonna defend yourself if you get into bother?" Winding down the rear window, the moustachioed Stanshall took a puff on a cigarette and exhaling into his face said, "Good manners."

End of encounter.

Although we were both beginning to sound a bit like John Wayne on LSD, we were now visiting the 'store', not the supermarket and getting the 'elevader', not the damn lift. The whole idea was to remain totally British throughout and just rely on the American fascination with our accents and way of doing things.

Despite the locals regularly asking, "Gee what part of Australia are you from?" we were gradually being accepted into the Hollywood way. Deep down though, deep inside we were British through and through, making regular forays to far flung LA locations to purchase Coleman's Mustard, Heinz beans and Tony Hancock records, just to regain some internal sanity.

The other bit of banter I loved was, "Gee where are you guys from?"

"England," I'd reply. "Well, what part?"

"All of me," I'd reply – knowing it would take a few minutes for them to get the gag.

Make no mistake though, Hollywood was a lonely place. You were there for one reason and one reason only - to make it in the industry. But of course, one never knew what was around the corner or how serendipity would catch you unawares!

Denise was a lovely lady who was a pal of my good Radio One matey, Richard Skinner. He'd told me to look her up when I got there as she was now single and on-the-look-out. We dated - there was no spark as such but she was a lovely lady and that was that.

It was a typically stinkingly hot Californian afternoon as I plodded wearily home along Sunset, fresh from yet another audition that was going to make me the biggest thing in Hollywood since Errol Flynn's willy.

As I turned left onto Le Brea, there in the parking lot outside my favourite 'liquor store' was Denise loading her car with groceries. "Hey you," she sparked, "Wahtcha doin?"

As we chatted, I was aware of scuffling noises in another car next to hers, and as I spun around, I could see a pair of legs dangling out of the driver's side. I suddenly had the strangest sensation; a tingle ran up and down my spine. As I stood there and stared - those legs! SO familiar!

"Hey Catherine," bawled Denise, "Come and meet Steve."

She was beautiful. Blonde hair dripping onto her shoulders and the biggest girly grin I'd ever seen. Two days later we met for dinner. A week later we were in love. A month later, she introduced me to her 23-year-old son, Damian. It transpired he was her son by Denny Laine, and she'd been in a band called Airforce with him back in the late 1960/70s.

It was a few weeks later she revealed all about that 'Airforce' gig, and that I was now in love with The Silver lady, the girl from that festival all those years before.

It was hard to take in. Now I was living with ex-Moody Blue, Denny Laine's ex-wife, direct from my bedroom wall.

It was now January 1990. I'd had a pretty rough Christmas, as in no TV or acting jobs to look forward to, and Catherine and I had sold Christmas trees up near the Hollywood sign to earn a few dollars.

It was straight back to the hustle on the twenty-sixth as the Americans rightly don't celebrate Boxing Day, and Ken was trying to hook up with an old pal, Maurice White, of Earth Wind & Fire, and was excited he was coming round for tea later that month. I was still in a spin, avoiding acting class like the plague and drinking like a fucking fish.

In fact, we both were – and one of our favourite things was to go shopping at the local supermarket, Walmart, for the groceries and as many vats of pink blush wine that we could carry. I'd often fill his trolley with condoms, tampons and all sorts of shite that he'd put onto checkout and he the same with me. It took our minds off everything.

Returning home after one particularly gruelling and fruitless audition, as I clicked the key into the lock, I could smell smoke. A sure sign the human chimney was at home. The lounge was empty, the bathrooms too. Nothing in his room I could see. A quick glance at the veranda outside left me puzzled where the hell he'd gone. I poured a drink and made a quick call to Catherine, opened some mail and submerged myself onto the huge sofa and turned on the TV. After around fifteen minutes I realised he still wasn't around – yet I could still smell ciggie smoke. Again, I did the rounds, but nothing.

I showered, then stepping into a humongous, recently nicked, hotel bathrobe I reached for my wardrobe door to get a clean shirt. There was Ken. Naked. Cigarette in hand. "Ullo Babe," he said casually. He stepped out and headed for his room. I fell to my knees and laughed more than I had for a very long time.

Determined to get my own back, dramatic measures were called for.

Ken had been in Vegas for a few days with a client and I was really looking forward to seeing the old twat as it was very lonely in there. As I greeted him at the door, I was brimming with sheer joy. "Ullo Babe," he said. "Ullo Babe, welcome home." As he went to his room, I could not contain my glee as I awaited the response.

"AAAAAARRRGH" was the start of it. Then it got loud.

I had taken half of the furniture in the flat and assembled it on his bed as a huge towering sculpture that went to the ceiling. Therefore, every time either of us came home, there would be another 'domestic work' piled up in each other's rooms or the dining table or pretty much anywhere. Every time I left the house. I'd always discover some vegetables or bananas in my case at some point during the day. This behaviour not only kept us amused – it kept us sane.

In fact, on one visit back to Blighty, it was only on opening my suitcase at Maggie's Islington flat that I discovered I'd transported a huge sack of potatoes home with me.

We also went for ridiculous crazed drunken road trips. This rather risky experience ended one day when we went to Malibu for a few Bloody Marys and ended up both asleep on the car roof on a side road off the highway!

Ken was also supremely anal about cleanliness in the apartment, and totally OCD, as in arranging things in order, even the magazines had to be fanned out 'just so'!

The best one, I think, was when he'd finished re-cleaning every nook and cranny for the fourteenth time that week. He saw me putting some rubbish into the kitchen waste bin. "Oy Babe," he yelled, "Don't put anything in that - I just emptied it."

Ken Gold. What a wonderful and very silly man. I'll always love him to bits.

CHAPTER 42

The Silver Wedding

Catherine and I married eighteen months later. This was to be her third marriage and she was to become the first Mrs Blacknell! I became more and more convinced that there were forces at work here that I had no control or say in. Catherine and I were – as most couples do as they near the hallowed event - shitting ourselves.

Catherine was best mates with mega-stars Melanie Griffith and Don Johnson and they needed a home for their super sweet Yorkshire Terrier called Gabriella.

When offered to adopt her, we gleefully accepted. Within a day or two both us were totally enamoured with our new addition.

Gabby went mental at the merest hint of an outside presence. So, at a knock on the door, amidst the voluminous yapping, one day, I opened the door.

"Surprise, surprise!" It was the bonkers bulk of Pedro.

My mind flashed back twenty years as the colours came and swirled across my eyes. My darling Pedro had now morphed from a cloaked man of mystery into a decloaked larger version of himself.

"Aaaaargh! What the fuck are you doing here?"

"I've come for your wedding," he announced. The great fool had just got on a plane and flown the 5,488 miles to be the best man he'd always wanted to be.

Pedro is the kind of friend that's hard to find.

"But it's in ten-days-time," shrieked Catherine.

The stupid idiot had got his timing wrong. She was fuming as we had to find a cheap shit hotel for the twat, which added to the overall pressure of it all. Gotta love him though.

In true American style the wedding was to be in a non-denominational church right there in West Hollywood.

The wedding day had arrived.

The term lead balloon comes to mind, but Catherine was indeed a rarity – an ironic American!

Still prone to the odd pill, Pedro had brought his own supply of legal medication. He was on placebo diamorphine for his constant body pain. He was not a well man to be honest, but I thought it would be rude if I didn't accept a few of those little white devils to stave off the nerves. Three of the little buggers and a huge swash of cheap shit Sunset Strip brandy and I was ready to go.

The service was conducted in front of family and friends. Ken was there, my sister too, and a collection of oddballs from Catherine's clan. Catherine's eccentric father, Bob, had made it, but also made it clear he wouldn't be coming to the reception as he didn't want to drink and drive.

The 'Vicar' was dressed as Elvis.

As we strode up the aisle, he started playing his guitar and attempting to sing. It was painful. I, though, was pain-free by now with my limbs shaking in jellied bliss.

I don't remember a thing until we arrived at our reception venue. It was the house and garden of one Pamela Des Barres – or 'Miss Pamela' as she was affectionally known to the world. She was the groupie Queen of Hollywood and shared her house in Santa Monica with a bizarre chap called Victor Hayden.

I was baffled that he had ten identical suits to wear 24/7 and slept with his boots on in case there was an earthquake. As they say over there, 'go figure.'

He had introduced her to his cousin, Don van Vilet, better known as the OTT, off-the fucking wall, alternative rockstar Captain Beefhart, who I still loved to listen to.

One of the Captain's best ever quotes was, "There are only forty people in the world and five of them are hamburgers!" A complete utter nutter. Very LA and VERY cool!

Thereafter, Pamela went on to spend time in and out of bed with the rock elite – everyone from Mick Jagger to Jim Morrison and Waylon Jennings. She then became rock royalty as one of Frank Zappa's girl band, 'The GTO's' Girls Together Outrageously, and as part of the infamous and late 'Cynthia Plaster Caster's' team, who were the super groupies of the day – where after shagging said rockstar would make a plaster cast of their chopper to preserve forever in the public eye.

In fact, Pamela once hailed her friend and peer in penis admiration as the 'Michaelangelo' of sex, drugs, and rock'n'roll.

Catherine and Pamela were best pals, so when Pamela offered to have the wedding afters at her Santa Monica home, it was a no brainer. Denise was there too, and Pamela's lovely other half, Michael 'Mikey' Des Barres, who'd risen to fame as part of rock dynamos Silver Head and Duran Duran break-off band, Power Station, as well as being a TV regular in Macgyver and on the silver screen. Victor was also there and a whole bunch of folks I'd never met. So, there I was, a bloke from Dartford – mixing with all these people. I was in heaven.

I was also in a right flipping state.

My turn came to give a little speech. I had rehearsed something light and short, but as I was finding it hard to stand up and talk at the same time, I had that sinking feeling that I was going to put my giant stupid foot in it.

"Well, my old friend, Richard Skinner, told me that when I got to Hollywood, I should look up Denise." I spluttered, "So I looked up her and didn't like what I saw!" Gasps ran around the room.

I had that horrid feeling when you want to run away and hide under the nearest rock.

With Denise in a flurry and a look from the new Mrs B to melt The Arctic - exit one back-pedalling mumbling mess to the back garden

Pedro, Ken, and Tobbe soon arrived and found me in a heap. The pills and brandy cocktail were still burning my brain and I was finding it hard to take in what I'd just done.

The garden was seething with the hippest hop of the Hollywood scene. I began to chat with Victor and other Magic Banders when I heard this sort of wailing voice behind them. It was full, loud and piercing. "Can't we ask that black bloke to bloody sit down," I said to Pamela.

"That black bloke is Arthur Lee," she snapped. It turned out he was the legendary Love frontman who was late sixties musical royalty. It was dawning on me more and more what I had actually landed myself in.

I was now aware of Catherine's celebrity status too, as she'd lived with Mick Jagger in London and dated the A-Z of rock heroes. She'd been at the piano with Clapton when he wrote *Layla*, knew Hendrix, Morrison and everyone on my bloody wall!

I was the newbie. Well, I was known on both coasts and beyond for *London Calling* of course – so I was no beginner, but, in Hollywood terms, I was one of a zillion trying to make it.

With all my new responsibilities, and as my savings dwindled to near zero, it became clear that I needed a job.

CHAPTER 43

Melrose Madness

Catherine had a lovely little shop on the super-trendy Melrose, deep in the heart of West Hollywood – as did manager Trish only a few blocks away – which sold rock and roll gear. It was the London equivalent of Kings Road.

It was a haven for everything trendy with a plethora of clothing stores / tattoo parlours and bars just oozing youth in every conceivable way.

'The Rockstore' was situated close to where West Hollywood bled into what was then Indian territory where commerciality ends and the harsh reality of poverty and gangland set in. One had to be very, very careful in daylight - let alone at night!

Catherine knew the owner. Paul was an amazing character. He was maniacally and, somewhat disturbingly, obsessed with collecting rock memorabilia to the point that his home a few blocks away - a huge rambling affair - was stuffed floor to ceiling with cardboard cut outs of Waylon Jennings, gold discs from REM, Rod Stewart's driving licence, Alice Cooper's toe nail clippings, and Debbie Harry's nipple rings, in fact anything that held this crazy man's interest.

The store itself was rammed with a zillion magazines / badges / posters. My God, the amount of posters! It was full and busy at the front, but 'out back' it was a jungle of unfiled paraphernalia and general mess.

He also had a 'mad' wife. I'd heard about Christine - a bit of a handful I was told.

I went to see Paul and was impressed with his inexhaustible knowledge of all things rock and roll. He was tall, paunchy, prone to bellowing rather than laughing and worryingly so sometimes. We got on great and I was introduced a few days later to the rest of the sales crew.

Motley? Oh yesssss.

Bill, or Swilve as we called him, was a bright pony-tailed young musician chappie with aspirations to setting up a record label. Tony was an actor, slight, very gay and very bulimic.

Tall, balding Eric was hard to figure, bumbling about, guffawing, a Trekkie and moody as the bluest blue. Jennifer was a round figured young girl, prone to shouting the wrong thing at the wrong time, and Rogers, a tall lanky streak of Mississippi piss, lean with blonde hair, he had dreams of playing guitar in a rock and roll band.

And there was me, now 38 and considered by them an old man.

There were, oddly, never many customers as it traded mostly on mail order. Often there'd be four of us, seated around the perimeter, perched over glass cases or sometimes just sitting on the huge floor and bagging magazines or packing up goods. The pay was $125 a week-ish. Depending on the hours and, although it didn't seem a lot, that was America. I could buy a steak and a beer for $5 whereas back home it was a lot more. So, it suited me! But it came at a price! As the store was hardly ever bothered by customers, a whole heap of mischief would go on and as the newcomer, I was an easy target.

The first Saturday shift was quite a busy affair and, exhausted, I piled into the remains of my car eager to get home and get something down my throat. A beer would be a good start.

As I creaked out of the car lot, there in line saluting were Bill, Eric, and Rogers. As I made it onto the main street, I could hear the sound of laughter mingled with a sort of clanking noise. Thinking that the wheels had fallen off, I stopped and on investigation found three lots of cans tied to my back axle. This then became a regular trick we'd pull on each other.

We'd lock each other out the back for hours on end, call from the phone box outside pretending to be a big buyer, and get them to go out the back looking for a poster we didn't have. An endless list of jokes and pranks. It was hilarious, we laughed all day and every day.

When Paul was away, we'd treat it like our house and call all and sundry down to the store, which occasionally backfired when he presented us with a phone bill.

It was chaos, regularly exacerbated by the regular, end of the day visit from his good lady, wine bottle in hand from yet another day's drinking at her clothing store a few doors away.

The combination of her and the meek but menacing frame of hubby, complete with her yapping dog, was worthy of a movie pitch. But they were very kind to me and I have to say to this day I can cut a mean cardboard box!

During this time, I was still going to auditions and attempting to take acting class. However, I just couldn't bring myself to go. What a twat!

I was quite relaxed doing the menial stuff at the store and, in fact, rather worryingly started to enjoy making up those bloody boxes.

One sunny day in May that all stopped. There I was cross-legged on the floor, attempting to cut down a larger box into a smaller one, when I looked to see the figure of me old DJ chum from London, Gary Crowley.

"What the FUCK are you doing here?" I yelled.

"And what about you?" he laughed.

Still reeling from that most awkward moment, I was again on the floor a few days later when once more I looked up and there standing, complete in black hat and cape, was Cult frontman, Ian Astbury. "Blacknell?"

"Yes," I whispered nervously. These were not the Hollywood moments I'd anticipated. What WAS I doing there?? With wings well and truly clipped, my confidence dropped like a stone. I suddenly felt vulnerable.

Perhaps the craziest night of all was when Catherine had invited Roger Daltrey and his lovely wife Heather to dinner. She'd introduced them many years before, and now they'd been married forever.

Just months before we'd stayed with them in their very English Sussex abode. I recall driving into the estate and seeing a little man standing on a rock – gazing out into the blue yonder. I'd never met him before, but had known Pete Townshend for years and knew a few bits about him. "So how much of that is yours?" I said gazing out to open fields and the horizon.

"All of it," he said.

Night soon followed with us sitting drinking, he quite enamoured with the thought of me playing Keith Moon in an upcoming movie venture. Needless to say, it never happened but some dreams take a while and never quite end up how you imagine them anyway.

The night they came to dinner I should never have told the boys that Mr and Mrs Daltrey were our guests.

After a few drinks and catch ups, we sat down to eat. Catherine, as a cook was quite something. As the food was being served, I could hear some noises outside, but Gabby the dog was in and I just thought it must be kids or something.

I was facing the outer ground floor window with our guests with their back to it. As Roger raised his glass in yet another toast, I then spied Bill and Rogers at the window; Bill in curly wig swinging a microphone on a long lead around his head; Rogers straddling his guitar à la Townsend.

I was speechless and kept the lip on the upper until they left heaving with laughter.

Bill later realised his dream and went on to co-found the super successful Side One Dummy label, while Rogers joined the ill-fated Blind Melon band.

It was so different to back home. These West Coasters don't muck about. Unlike the British, who take years to call people a friend, out there it was simply a case of (once more) not being a twat and then you'll be okay. Well, it seemed I'd been taken into the fold.

Things started to happen and, in a few months, I'd bagged three national TV commercials! For eye glasses, the national lottery and, lo and behold, Diet Coke as a film director on a beach!

In all three I played my big nosed, bumbling CLEEESSE-alike character and all seemed to be going great. A veritable piece of piss, thought I. What was all the fuss about? But filming an ad is one thing, it actually surfacing on air is another thing entirely.

I was flown out to Florida to shoot the ad, complete with my own caravan I might add, a fact that was not lost on my now burgeoning ego. I'd shot around sixty takes of me on a crane, shouting "CUT!" That was it. That was my only line! A piece of PISSSSS!

Back in Hollywood I was summoned to a studio in Burbank to shout 'Cut' again in as many different ways as my mouth and throat could manage.

The initial pay was around a thousand dollars, plus expenses. But, of course, it all relied on repeat fees and the size of the TV audience. You can imagine how, as they say stoked/excited/buzzed I was!

I was then told that it was to be shown at half time in the Superbowl! This was mega bucks and suddenly the sign on the hill started to glow with gold, and a huge dollar sign arose in my brain. I'd done it!

Dick Van Dyke, eat your chuffing heart out! With two days to go, Trish and I were nervous wrecks.

It was a HUGE deal, and the more we thought about it, the bigger it felt. The other two accompanying ads had screened in local states by then, but THIS was the biggie.

"It's off," came the voice of my William Morris secret agent - we called them secret as we could never ever track them down.

"Off?" I screamed. "Yeh, they scrapped the ad, Steve. But hey - there'll be more."

As I plonked the phone down, I didn't realise that was to be the first of a slew of near misses that would characterise the next year or two.

Although I had thousands of hours of screen time behind me, it was all TV stuff. Acting was a different kettle of fish entirely. I tried a few weeks at *The Groundlings*, an 'improv' group on Melrose that had spawned the likes of the infamous American clown, Pee-wee Herman, but I hated it, and I was crap too. Despite protestations from Trish and other supporters, I steadfastly refused to take my class and insisted that my Englishness and brazen self could and would carry me to the top. I should have worn a baseball cap with a big T on the front for 'TWAT'.

As acting agencies go, they don't get much bigger than CAA - the Creative Artists Agency – looking after everyone from Cruise to De Niro, the Pope to God and four of his disciples.

Trish, once more, had a contact and, hey presto, I had a one to one with a Vice Chairman of Talent Acquisition or some such preposterously named position.

As I had a history of sight-reading scripts, I was actually quite adept at getting one for the first time and reeling off a pretty cool read. This obviously went down well with the titled man as, two weeks later, Trish informed me that a certain 'exec' wanted to see me.

I couldn't sleep for days. I lay awake thinking what it could be.

He was the big cheese of something or other and, as if in the wave of a wand, I found myself suited and booted once more in front of this cigar-smoking giant of a man.

"Steve," he boomed. "We see you have tremendous energy. We see you are a cross between Rahbin Willams and Jahhhn Cleeesss. You are a real one off."

'Oh, here we bleeding go again!' I screamed within.

"Buttttt," he grunted as he strode up and down in front of his ginormous walnut wooded desk. "We feel at this time that we do not have the machinery in place to facilitate such a combustive energy as yours and it entails untold resources to bring your inestimable talents to fruition."

He puffed away furiously as he stared at me through the smoke.

"So, is it a no?" I ventured.

"Yes," he said. "But the door is always open." Dumbfounded, I clambered into the waiting Land Rover. "Oh, sod it," yelled Trish. "Let's go home."

There, in all its glory was the Hollywood way. They didn't want to take a chance but were covering their arses just in case. All that wait, all that way, for a NO! Well, at least you can get through the door.

Well, Hulk got to make his first starring role in 1991 in the highly entertaining *Submarine Commando,* as Peter and chums began plotting my ascension to world domination.

All that sounded brilliant, but twat-face here was still refusing to take acting classes. Looking back, I was just being an arse. Out of my comfort zone, and petrified I'd fail. It's one thing being yourself on a TV screen, but another set of skills entirely inhabiting another persona. But I thought, stupidly, that I could pull it off.

Now, though fully fit, I was getting auditions by the bucketful in both voice-overs, ads and movies, so I was certain my break would come.

CHAPTER 44

Desert Island Dreams

I was now auditioning like mad. I'd go for anything and everything. I was in such a hurry to succeed they all faded into a blur.

I often got muddled up and went prepared for the wrong job. Not only was I not a very good actor, I was, in effect, a TV presenter being me - attempting badly to be other people, and I hated having to make any effort to dress as the character I was portraying. After mega moaning from the deadly duo of wife and manager, I succumbed and said I'd make more effort, and yes, "I'll be taking class soon."

I'd had a call from one of the secret agents about a great commercial gig. It was for band aids or plasters as they are better known to many. I read the brief open-eyed. This was the one I'd make an effort for. I needed to push myself a bit more.

There were of course many costume stores in Hollywood, and there was a good one at the beach. That was a bit of a generic term for Santa Monica/Venice and bits in between. A strange combo of the rich, the surfers and the down and outs. A real Californian Cocktail.

So, I rented the relevant uniform and arrived a half an hour early for the audition in the terminally trendy Beverly Hills. I had gone right over the top this time. I was dressed as well as any doctor in The Cedar Sinai. White coat, stethoscope, fake badge, glasses, pencils in pocket and clipboard in hand. I felt the bollocks. Crap at learning scripts, I was equally overjoyed with my pitiful three lines to make 'come alive' and be - me!

"Steve Blacknell?" came a strangled cry from the open studio door. With a pompous stride I'd rarely felt of late, I bounded in.

"Welcome, Steve," murmured an ungainly skinny chap sitting at a long plastic table.

"Not too certain about the outfit?"

Slowly I realised they were hurriedly looking down at their scripts and squinting back at me warily. Whether it was too many cheap beers on my part, or my agent back on the

Ketamine, I'll never know, but there were no doctors in the commercial, I'd been requested to be a New York cop. Whatever ego I had, was now flapping its wings and half way out of the window.

I read the part of the cop as Doctor sodding Kildare and got a smaller role as a drunk with one line. A result, but, as always, I'd walk away from these bizarre situations with one thought ringing in my brain. Only in Hollywood!'

I was now getting a few small roles – and small they were but not too taxing on my limited skills of learning lines. One of the best ever was spending a day with my hands down Leslie Nielsen's underpants.

It was the movie trailer of *Naked Gun 33/3*. I was playing his overtly gay butler, measuring him for his new suit and fawning over him like the star he was. I'd heard that Leslie was the consummate joker. He was. Upon entering his caravan on that first shooting day in Santa Monica, out came his warm and welcoming outstretched hand. A quick squeeze and a massive fart sound let rip! He loved his beloved fartbox and it accompanied him wherever he went. I'd always wondered about his serious side. As in, if he had one!

No problems making 'em laugh, but huge ones with his lines. Three words into a line to camera it was 'prompt', and this was a trailer! Gawd knows how long Airplane took to film.

It's often said that it takes an Englishman years to become a true friend. Yet in La La land you can meet a bloke in a bar and, all of a sudden, they are your best pal for a week or two, then that's that.

Dave Williams was a VP (Vice President) at the mammoth Disney Corporation. Amongst the piles of shite he had to deal with each and every day, there was always a bunch of resumés from would-be superstars. For some reason, God only knows how and why, mine popped up and caught his eye. He had been a devout fan of *London Calling* and was intrigued to see I'd finally made it across the water! Trish called me and said, "This guy you gotta meet!"

And so, we did. For 'caaaacktails' as they so lovingly describe anything remotely alcoholic in LA!

The Formosa Cafe had been around since 1925. It was, and still is, opposite the United Artists lot on Santa Monica Blvd. Attracting the likes of Humphrey Bogart and Clark Gable back in the day, with Sinatra reputedly spending hour upon hour there pining over Ava Gardner. It was luxuriously pokey, with a delicious rustic feel to it that bounced you back in time the moment you opened the door.

The head barman was a great chum of Catherine's, the magnificent Lindy Brewerton who had worked there for nigh on 50 years!! An endearing white-haired charmer who poured drinks so strong they blew your socks and shoes off. He was a real gent. He'd charge you a couple of dollars and always get huge tips. One day he said to me, "Stephen, I'll show you how to make the perfect vodka martini."

With that he produced a martini glass, dipped the rim into the crushed ice tray and rubbed the slightest trace of dry martini around the rim. He filled the glass with neat high explosive vodka and then, POW! It worked every time. Three of those and you were seeing Bogie and company in triple! He later wrote a stunning book called, 'Forty Years Behind Bars'. That was the wonderful Lindy.

The Formosa was where Dave and I first met, one dusky Saturday night. He was aware of what I was trying to do, to be the next JAHHHHHN CLEEEESE or Sellers etc. but aware, too, of my brayed 'Cockinese' accent.

He soon proved that was one obstacle that would NOT get in his way. After several meets, he confronted me with a most remarkable concept. He wanted to build my own desert island slap bang in the middle of Hollywood, complete with real sand and a watery waterfall! This was going to be a TV pilot and a half!

Desert Island Video was a weird and wacky cross between the infamous BBC Radio series *Desert Island Discs,* where celebs selected their own favourite songs to take to their island, and the comic castaway sitcom *Gilligan's Island,* with some celebs thrown in. In this case, hunky black heartthrob actor, Blair Underwood, the young chap from LA Law, the rock band, Cheap Trick, and a bizarre assortment of B-list names were signed up to the show!

The idea was that muggins here had been inexplicably stranded on a desert island, videos were being washed up on the shore and I'd take a look at them in my role as a former MTV VJ! Then I'd chat with my fellow island inhabitants, all at the frenetic Blacknell 'pace'.

Dave loved the accent and told me to stick with it. When asked what we should call the island, I immediately came up with 'No Man', which I thought was particularly clever. DW was half-Welsh and very Anglicised and got the gag, but I had severe problems explaining to the crew and guests that 'No Man Is an Island' was very funny indeed.

There I was, in Hawaiian shirt, shifting around a fake beach, rehearsing my lines when there was a big crashing sound. The air con had decided to pack up, leaving the set literally like the sun-drenched inferno it was meant to look like! Bearing in mind it was about ninety-five degrees outside, this felt hot!

Then it just got hotter and hotter. I've a history of hating the heat and have been known to pass out with a lack of air swirling around me. "Shove this for a game of soldiers," I thought. However, just for a change, I was the star of this 'ere show, so I had to behave like one.

Poor David was striding up and down, bellowing orders left and right, sweating like a pig on a spit and literally fuming! After all, this was HIS money, he'd raised just over a million dollars to get this far, and he could see it literally evaporating in front of his eyes.

As if matters couldn't get any worse, they then did. I'd called Trish to tell her of the problems on set and she demanded to talk to Dave. "I don't freakin' belieeeeeve it!" shrieked DW. "She's saying if I don't double your pay, you'll walk!" I was aghast. Dave and I were now firm friends and this was so out of the blue. I was choked. Having agreed to her demands we carried on.

We finished the day thinner than when we had started, but everyone agreed it had been a good one. The band and celebs were cool, and it was now for the next huge step. The edit.

Before that could be completed there was one 'exterior' that needed to be done. Catherine and I were dispatched to Hawaii with a film crew to shoot one shot of me emerging out of the water to my new home on 'Noman'. It was utter luxury. A suite in a top hotel in Maui, with enough Caaaacktales and lobster dishes to sink the ship I'd sunk in.

The shot was easy enough. Me... bedraggled and distraught, soaked to the skin - crawling out of the sea and collapsing on the beach. It seemed so easy. After around ten takes, we trekked back to hotel - yet more Caaaaaacktails and bed.

It felt like the big quake had finally hit the city when Dave called me a week later. It transpired that the director had failed to size up the shot properly. I was crawling out of the ocean, the only speck of human life to be seen, with an enormous great pylon in the background. I'd never heard David so mad. It was all unusable and thousands of his dollars sank down the tubes.

A few voice-overs from moi, and within three weeks we had a sizzle reel ready to go. That's American for demo, as in an edited version that runs for maybe 10-15 minutes tops.

I was then back at the Rockstore bagging magazines – with my dream a little nearer and my hopes a little higher.

Late one afternoon I was home on a day off when the doorbell rang. A delivery driver stood there. "Please sign here sir," he said, which I did. My gaze drifted over his shoulder to the bottom of the drive, where a big truck full of crates was parked. One after another were brought into the hallway, until before me stood fifteen crates of Heineken lager. The driver handed me a delivery note. "Guvner" by now my nickname from the team, 'This is to replace the liquid you lost, all my best, Dave.' It was there – right then - that I knew David Williams and I would be friends for a very long time.

Despite all David's efforts, the response to my machine gun patter Cockney didn't exactly set Tinseltown alight! But Dave ploughed on regardless.

I was sweeping the floor at the store late one Monday night. The phone, which hadn't rung for hours, burbled loudly. I grabbed at it, vacuum in hand. Instead of Joe Blow on the other end asking for a 1974 Rush poster, there came the sound of one very, very, excited half Welsh exec!

"Guvnor!" he loves it. He fucking loves it!!" yelled Dave down the blower. It transpired that an ex-colleague at Disney had forwarded it to a chum at Diet Coke.

"He says that Black-nell is going to be the new… guess what – freakin' Rahhhhbin Williams, and when he gets back from vacation, we are all meeting with a view to sponsorship."

THIS was it – at last! Yessssss!

For two weeks, I walked to and from work dreaming up merchandise spots and imagining being back on American TV.

Dave and I met over too many caaaaacktails and planned the ascent of Everest.

Catherine, a very wise Hollywood owl, was reserved about it all, telling me to calm down and not count my chickens, and stop jumping around like a big twat.

It was almost three weeks to the day that the phone went at home around 8am. Those calls are weird. You know it's either good news, bad news, or worse.

It was David.

“Guvnor, he's dead!”

“He's what?? WHO is?” I screamed.

“Chris that Diet Coke guy. He drowned in a surfboarding accent in Florida a week ago!”

Right then, right there and then, my mind sprang back to a famous Tony Hancock line – as he'd discovered that the last page was missing from his new mystery book. When Hancock asked his friend Sid what happened to the author? “Dead.” came the reply. “DEAD! THE FOOL!” came the laconic response.

And that's the only thing I could think. ‘DEAD!!! How could he?’

With his sad demise at the bottom of the sea, so sank the project, never to be seen or heard of again.

CHAPTER 45

Riverrrr-Red, Riverrr-Red!

Despite my continual knockbacks, Catherine was incredibly supportive. She knew Hollywood like the back of her dainty hand but I really had no clue. I was just sticking my big nose out there and seeing who might bite. I returned to my TV roots via a great friend of hers, Jack Gorton, a truly special soul. Laid back LA drawl, humour as dry as the desert and a genius on the quiet, he and his similarly ebullient pal, Bob Olive, were working on some project ideas and put me forward as the host of a brand-new talk show idea, '*Men in Suits Talking*'. He had sold the idea to MTM (Mary Tyler Moore's production company) but they were not that happy with my accent, so Jack had to audition about 40 others but finally gave me the job.

It was the Cleese shampoo saga all over again. Sometimes, though, you find something that's totally you.

I was to play the genial host to four top LA stand-ups including the future *Simpsons* producer, Dana Gould, and through gags we would explore the issues of the day.

We shot the pilot in a lovely little theatre off Sunset to a selected audience – and it rocked like a bobbing boat! Maybe THIS time.

It was torture waiting for MTM to make their minds up, but in the end, it appeared that a bunch of bastards had already put the same idea into production, and it surfaced on a comedy channel. Jack was beside himself and fumed for weeks on end, but again, in Hollywood anything goes!

Despite yet another blow to what was left of my ego, I was weirdly accumulating a legion of very unlikely fans in the shapes of a motley collection of Hollywood veterans! Robert Easton was already a Tinseltown hero through his appearances in everything from the early *Beverly Hillbillies* to the George Burns and Gracie Allen shows. The list was endless.

It was late one afternoon in his Hollywood home that I couldn't resist it. "Robert, that voice of yours, it's bugging me, what is it?" Peering at me through his flurry of white hair, he slowly, very slowly said, "Heeeyyy Troy."

It hit me like a sledgehammer. "Oh, Jeeeeezuz," I cried. As a lifelong fan of Gerry Anderson's *Stingray* puppet series, I immediately recognized him as Troy Tempest's Southern sidekick, 'Phones', I could not believe it. He'd reinvented himself in his later years as the white-haired, white-bearded professor of all 'things' speech.

Following the Desert Island flop, he the 'Dialect Doctor' was tasked to rid this wretched soul of all things *Cockinese*. It was a complete thrill to be working with the man behind one of my childhood heroes, who'd given Gregory Peck his German accent in the *The Boys from Brazil,* and worked with everyone from Ben Kingsley in *Ghandi* to Al Pacino's Cuban persona in *Scarface.* Now he was coaching little old Steve Blacknell. Sending me home after every lesson with the words Red River – River Red to say a zillion times as I padded my way around town, the intention being to train my tongue to roll my R's - to Americanise me. What a man. A complete legend and like so many – sadly missed!

Another fan, Kathy Freeman, was a Hollywood 'vet' who'd cut her comedic teeth in the early Jerry Lewis comedies of the 50s and 60s and weirdly went on to stardom in my two favourite movies, *The Blues Brothers*, as the sliding nun, and alongside George Kennedy and my old chum Leslie Neilson in *Naked Gun 33/3 The Final Insult.* I'll never forget Kathleen telling me that I was "So special" and to "Hang in."

Yet another was Marvin Kaplan, a total enigma. I'd been hired by the producer, Paul Flattery, who would later cast me in the Phil Collins video *Hang in Long Enough*, to star in a rather strange corporate movie for CBS. I played a doctor alongside another Hollywood regular in the balding moustachioed shape of one Niles Brewster with Marvin as the squinty-eyed potty professor.

Marvin was the amazing man who'd caused such a stir in his major debut with Spencer Tracey and Audrey Hepburn aged just 21 in the 1949 epic *Adam's Rib.* You'd recognise him from his great cameos in *It's a Mad Mad Mad World* and *The Great Race* and so many more.

Once more, something was bugging me. Where did I know that voice from? Before each take, he would look down at his hands and crease his failing eyes. Despite his ill health, his presence was incredible. He WAS Hollywood to the rest of the cast. Again, I was in total awe.

One day I summoned the courage to ask him if he was praying on set? “Nah,” he replied in that wondrous twangy droll tone. “I have my lines on the back of my hand.”

We began to get on as chums. I was in dreamland. This man was so respected in town, he was the Head of AFTRA, the big actors’ union, and he was formally in my corner.

Each night I'd get home and say to the Mrs, “It’s really bugging me. I need to know where I know that voice.” I was determined that next day I'd pluck up the courage. And so it was, as we ‘wrapped’ on the Friday in a hot sweaty set in Burbank, that I got Marvin alone in his dressing room and very, very shyly asked the question. “Marvin, I just have to know, that voice, where do I know it from?” With a huge sigh and a look that could have crossed an ocean, he had a sip of cold coffee and expelled thus... “How ya doin' TC?” For hecks sake. It was Choo Choo from *Top Cat*.

All this time I’d been working with one of my cartoon heroes who’d had pride of place on the bedroom wall in distant Dartford. I was flummoxed. In both shock and amazement, I sped home.

“It's him - it's him,” I spluttered to the wife. “It’s bleedin’ Choo Choo!”

What great company to be in. I was blessed.

CHAPTER 46

Geoff Hurst and Two World Wars

Having had the benefits of several months work with 'The Dialect Doctor' I felt equipped to take on the world with my brand-new American accent – I felt the universe was ready not for Steve BLACK-nell... but Steve Black-NELL in all my stateside glory.

Out of the blue – well, out of the smog – came a very odd call from The William Morris Agency asking if I could do my best Johnny Carson accent and host a TV game show pilot in... Germany!

Excitedly, I agreed – bursting to show that bit of the world how Americanised I'd become.

It was called *'The News Quiz'* to be filmed in a cute little studio affair in downtown Cologne and within a week I was planted in my very Germanic hotel under the name Steve Black-NELLLLL.

I was already trying out my new found mother tongue. At dinner that first night... "Hi, can I get a steak – rare to medium, fries, two eggs sunny side up and... I'll order my Caaaacktail in a few."

It all sounded quite good – rather swell... I chuckled to myself.

Next day I was Red Riverrrr Redding on the 'john' (the poopoo place) and continued nigh on rupturing my twisting tongue in the cab on route to the studio.

The show was pretty standard really. Two teams of motley assorted volunteers who'd answer questions on world news – with meself as the 'moderator' – a term they'd nicked from the States as if to underpin their ambitions to sell the bugger both domestically and globally.

All I could think was, 'Remember that I was American to the core and don't mention Geoff Hurst or two World Wars', and so the camera rolled.

"Hi everyone... I'm Steve Black-NELL," I said, "And a huuuge welcome to the Nooooze Kwiz."

So far so good – as I felt Eric the Endorphine start another epic journey up my spinal column.

This was a piece of Germanic piss.

It was fortunate that my hosting skills were on automatic as we sailed through the first thirty minutes with Johnny here holding the proceedings together nicely – and my 'R' sound intact.

I just about managed to keep in character throughout the lunch break and was raring to go.

About ten minutes in there was a loud clunk from above and a gantry came crashing down, knocking over a camera or two and everything ground to a halt. It was now about 6pm German time and we all had to vacate while things were fixed.

It transpired that the air conditioning was now out of action, and it was some three very, very sweaty hours later that we were called back in to a now boiling studio.

Now knackered I was sounding a bit 'mid-adlandic' as my 'R's' were gradually disappearing up my arse.

As we re-commenced, I could feel that something was up as, although the show was in full flow, my accent was literally melting away.

With more technical issues along the way – we were now massively overrunning and as the minutes ticked by, so I could feel Black-NELL gradually reverting to a totally exhausted BLACK-nell

So, by the time we got to the bye-byes, I was back in full blown Cockinese

"And that's it for now", I blurted. "We'll see ya again soon. Ta Ta!" And with a bye-bye gesture it was over.

It was all weirdly quiet as polite applause rippled around the set, and that was that.

I said my farewells in an accent half-way to Lewisham and back.

A few weeks later, I was back home in Hollywood with the producer on the blower.

"How was it," I asked with a lump in my throat.

"Well... it was sort of okay," she mumbled.

'Ah', I thought – maybe they'd been able to get over the last bit when I became English again.

"I'm afraid we may have to redo some stuff, especially the ending," she said.

Puzzled, I couldn't think why.

It transpired that amidst the heat and my failing accent, in waving goodbye, I had motioned the Hitler salute to camera.

She was a mad mix of disdain and stifled laughter. Enough to say I wasn't called back to do any more and that was it.

As they say in Germany, 'Vielleicht sollte ich einfach ich selbst bleiben' (maybe I should stick to being me!).

CHAPTER 47

Our Man in Hollywood!

The late and great Francis Megahy was a character in every sense of the word. He was a legendary TV director and had helmed the *Minder on The Express*, amongst others, and I'd connected with him via some old pals back home at the BBC and the *Top of The Pops* crowd. He was a long-time partner of the legendary Flick Colby of Pan's People.

We'd meet at the illustrious Barney's Beanery and talk TV turkey. Over a month or two, and enough beer to sink the Titanic again, we evolved a plan for a TV show. But we felt my time had, maybe, finally come and *Our Man in Hollywood* was born!

The premise was not exactly the most original in broadcasting history. It was, basically, a Yankee in King Arthur's Court in reverse – in other words, it was a wacky Brit running around Tinseltown open-mouthed, aghast at the glitter and gold-plated sidewalks.

The great thing was that Francis was very well connected and so my guests were very often pure gold themselves. Drinks with Bob Hope? Oh, go on then.

So, when he said, "Do you fancy a day with Dudley Moore?" Well, I flipped my flipper!

My late dear dad had bought me the then outrageous Peter Cook and Dudley Moore '*Goodbyee*' single from Challenger & Hicks record shop in Dartford when I was 13 in 1965. I adored it. Never, ever, did I imagine that one day, sometime in the future, I'd actually meet that short-arsed genius on a set in Hollywood. He, like so many others, had adorned that bedroom wall. Again, here I was meeting my heroes. This was now getting all a bit weird.

And so, we met Dud. I spent a brilliant unforgettable day just chatting on and off camera about life, music, and Peter Cook. Whizzing from location to location on the back of a truck thing. He was everything and much more than I'd imagined.

In actuality, he was just like showbiz stars should be - nice, polite, and interested to hear about me. It's very weird that we seem conditioned to think that celebrities by default are self-imploding fuckwits. 'You'll never guess, I met that Steve McQueen once and he said 'hello' and asked how I was!' But of course, they should do that, they are people who took another trail in life that led them to be in the public eye. They *should* be courteous and kind, like we all should. It never fails to amaze me how a celebrity saying 'hello' can be considered an anomaly. We expect them to be offish and tight lipped. So very strange.

Nothing ever became of *Our Man in Hollywood.* It melted away and joined the thousands upon thousands of pilots that had crashed into the sea of nothingness. But maybe there was still hope out there. I would lie awake at night wondering if it really was worth all this effort. At least Catherine was a realist. She'd seen it all a zillion times before, but like Trish and the agents, they all gave me great support.

The Dead Poets Society had been a major movie classic in 1989 and earned Robin Williams an Oscar nomination. It was to be made into a TV series. I'd now got a slight reputation as 'That mad Brit' and with nothing to lose, auditioned for the lead role as the eccentric English teacher, John Keating, that Williams had nailed so amazingly.

I was offered the part at the Beverley Hills Hotel by one of Disney's top bods!! Again, this seemed too good to be true and the project was shelved. I followed this up by securing the role of the butler in Francis Ford Coppola's 1992 blockbuster, Bram Stoker's *Dracula*, before the part was scrapped three weeks before filming!

So near but not even the distant faintest whiff of a cigar!

Things momentarily looked up when, out of the blue, I was given a small role in *Hollywood Blvd 2,* another dollar friendly venture from the master of corn and catastrophe himself, Roger Corman! The role was a dodgy gambler type called Steve.

So excited, I waited eight and a half hours on the set for my one scene. This time I actually spat out my three lines, and to my amazement I was summoned to see the man himself. "You're a good young talent," he mumbled. Praise indeed. But later, in relative tranquillity, I wondered if that might have been a backhanded compliment as amongst his fifty-five films as director and three hundred and eighty-five as producer, including such gems as *Attack of the Crab Monsters*, *The Saga of The Viking Women & Their Voyage to The Waters of The Great Sea Serpent*, and *Slumber Party Massacre II*, I had that cringy crawly feeling that my talents may have been more suited to the above. Despite my negativity, I was beginning to feel that maybe, just maybe, I was a good fit for the peculiar Hollywood way.

Sitting out on our garage roof on a Sunday afternoon with potent $1.35 beers in hand and the Eagles blaring out on the radio, I felt that maybe the USA would be my forever home. I'd always detested the *Hotel California* mob but there's a whole lot of difference listening to them on a rainy day in Bexleyheath than speeding down the Pacific Coast Highway in ninety-degree heat or sunning myself on our garage roof.

CHAPTER 48

The Romanian Bends

It was another day in Hollywood.

Catherine shouted excitedly, “Peter's on the phone!”

Peter Young, or Peedeee as I now knew him from Gersh, seemed excited!

“Hey, BlackNELL.”

I was Steve Black-NELL again. I dunno – we gave them the language and all they do is screw it up.

It appeared someone had dropped out of an on-the-face-of-it high-end romp called *Secret of The Ice Cave*. It starred Michael Moriarty, who I knew from Clint Eastwood's classic cowboy flick, *Pale Rider*. He'd won some Emmys too. There was also one of my great lady fantasies, the salubrious Sally Kellerman. My Dartford wall had a picture of the entire cast of her and the rest of Altman’s legendary Korean War romp, *MASH* – where she was Oscar nominated for her role as Hot Lips O'Houlihan and trod some very big footsteps for Loretta Swit to follow some four years later on the smaller screen. At eighteen years of age, she looked untouchable and a true star. Could I actually meet her?

To add to the excitement of the occasion, the whole thing was to be shot in Chile!

Hurried calls home followed. Maybe THIS was it! I had the eighth lead. My biggest role so far, and more lines than I was used to. A couple of pages worth and three scenes! This whole treasure-seeking yarn saw me as Billy, the loud cockney drugged-up manic English twit who also flew planes for a living. “Just be yourself,” said Peedee down the phone.

Well, for someone who acted exactly the same character in every damn role, that might not prove too difficult! I think if I was cast to play a one-legged German pirate, I'd still play it as an out-of-control cockney twat. I'd always thought that if I was a good presenter, I'd easily adapt to this acting lark. But as clever clogs here STILL refused acting ‘class' it was no wonder I couldn't tell the difference! All I needed was an autocue on set and I know I'd stand a better chance at success. No such luck.

Picking up my 'sides', the script with your bits frenziedly highlighted in yellow marker pen, it appeared I was to be flying a plane and actually dying into the bargain a bit later in the proceedings.

This, supposedly glossy, *Indiana Jones* type spectacular began to shed said gloss after I was politely told I wouldn't meet Sally or Michael as they were shooting on different days.

'Ah well,' I thought, 'at least I'll be up there on screen with her.'

I was to work mainly with a lovely young lad called David Mendenhall, who'd secured his place in movie history playing opposite Sylvester Stallone in the handily rhymed 1987 flop, *Over the Top*, a truly awful affair that would only pale in awfulness to this rancid Cannon Films rework of every bad movie known to man. It had to be said though that David, who again played the boy hero, was darn good in it, and we struck up a great kinship during our time there.

"Just be yourself, Steve," Peedee's words of discomfort kept banging around my brain. So, I was!

I was filming one day in an old airfield in the quaint yet dilapidated town of Orsono, 'flying' a stationary plane supposedly belting through the clouds at the speed of light. I was meant to be coked-up and on a mission to... somewhere - I can't even remember... but I was definitely on a mission!

The 'renowned' Romanian director, Radu Gabrea, sadly no more, but a jolly, friendly chap had given me threadbare directions to "go nuts". Bringing my similarly skimpy range of acting talent into play, I thought, 'Think Dudley Moore, what would he do?' That loveable sketch with him and Peter Cook singing '*Goodbyee'*, sprung to mind with Dudley's crazed goofy expressions. And that was what I did. They loved it! I'm doing alright here, I mused that night in one of the shabbiest hotels I've ever been in, let alone slept in.

Bristling with the buzz of it all, amidst a new found air of confidence, I awoke the next morning with a decided spring in my step. This acting lark's a piece a piss, I thought as I turned up for my final scene. I'd been so carried away with my aerial antics that I'd actually forgotten that this was the bit that I crashed the plane and dutifully passed away amidst the flames, last dying breath etc.

Now I'd been good at the manic bit, with Dudley to spirit me on, but my face and testicles fell when Radu informed me of what was to come. I had some fucking dreadful lines, something like "Find them and you'll inherit five million dollars," or some shit. Anyhow, it suddenly hit me that this would be *real acting*. Fumbling through the remnants of my mind, I was struggling to picture a dramatic actor who could help me through this nearing crisis. All I could see was Tommy Cooper, Stan Laurel, and oh, for shits sake Dudley shitting Moore!

"ACTIONNNN," yelled Radu. In that moment, I knew just how much I should have taken my acting class. I had nothing. Fuck all to fall back on, my mind a complete blank.

I delivered my lines with all the aplomb of a tuneless choirboy and I could feel the atmosphere chill around me. With the camera about six inches from my slowly closing eyes, as I gasped my last breath, it felt like someone or something had REALLY died.

"CUUTTTT!!!" he screamed, as I slowly opened one eye, then the other. I could see him walking slowly to a nearby fence, and slowleeeee, very slowleeee he leant over it and I could hear him gently weeping and grunting into his sleeve.

It was then that I realised that the only thing that had died there was my career.

I've always called it the 'Romanian Bends'. That saddest picture ever is of a director, full of hope, on a crap movie with a crap budget, bent double as despair bubbles explode with a really, really crap actor.

Next day I was on my way back home to Hollywood with deep thoughts about now getting acting lessons, which, of course, I never ever took.

There then followed a bizarre week in which I played a scene with Jamie Lee Curtis, for a new soap, as her young lover, and had to shove my tongue right down her lovely skinny throat.

Plus, a fascinating morning with my glove puppet, Sooty, who I used as a prop in a TV pilot with Henry '*The Fonze*' Winkler who offered to buy the fading ted, but NOT for sale matey.

I didn't get either gig, but I did get a cold sore from Jamie Lee, and Sooty, as ever, said not a sodding word.

CHAPTER 49

Oh No… It's Bob!

Catherine had lived a remarkable life, as would be chronicled later in her 2007 autobiography, *Dandelion* – where I make a brief appearance. As Diane Keaton's movie double, she followed in the footsteps of her rather unique father's career choices.

As one critic concluded on her life story, 'Her supremely dysfunctional family will remain with you long after you've finished this book'.

I'd already had my share of them, but the ladder of dysfunctionality was endless.

This was Hollywood though.

Catherine's mother had been a folk singer whose aunt was once married to legendary Hollywood producer, Busby Berkeley. But her adoring father, Bob, was another thing altogether.

An ex-racing driver, who had raced with Mario Andretti back in the day, he'd been George C. Scott's double in several of the great man's best works so, when Scott retired, Bob went into stunt drinking, and rather unfortunately changed his sexuality. In fact, he was a full-on transexual, way ahead of his time.

I first encountered him high above the Hollywood polluted clouds as Catherine pointed out a zig-zag plume of white smoke phutting over Sunset and Highland. The phone whirred into action.

"It's Bob," she mouthed. "He's up to his old tricks again." Bob was a qualified pilot and loved flying up from his Palm Springs fortress with enough alcohol in him to knock out an army. I could hear him hissing to her. "Father, please go back home," was all the Mrs could mutter.

I'd only really spoken to him once on the phone.

Convinced that he would make an effort for his new son-in-law, Catherine insisted we should take a weekend break with him so we could 'connect'. Palm Springs itself was, and I assume still is, a glossy manicured retirement home stuck in the middle of the Colorado desert's Coachella Valley, just over a hundred miles away from the buzz of LA. Average age ninety-nine, and the place to slow down, take it easy and pass away far from the public eyeball.

We were greeted that memorable Saturday night by what can only described as a mess of a man. Spindly, with a podgy gut, a slightly newtish spine, and eyes that seemed to belong somewhere else, he was dressed in a long blue skirt with tights and slippers.

His face was like a movie.

A horror movie.

Dribbling onto his frilly shirt, he welcomed us clutching a huge tumbler of orange juice that reeked of neat booze. Still in shock, he led us into his vast bungalow festooned with obscure World War II posters, the house in chaos. In disbelief, we were shown to our guest room that consisted of two collapsible chairs with blankets on. We had brought Gabby along for the ride as always, when she suddenly let out a large yelp!

In walked Bob, pulling something behind him. As he sat down, in full view came the extraordinary sight of his pet sausage dog. But this was a dog with a difference. The poor thing had only two front legs and Bob had attached his two rear stumps to a cart with two back wheels.

I was beginning to feel a little uneasy… what, where was I? Who WAS this fruitcake? Answer? My freakin' father-in-law!

After an excruciating night at one of his local bar hangouts, where he proceeded to drink and dribble his way through the evening with a bunch of his cronies, it was mercifully home time and the sanctity of 'bed'!

After a few hours we both drifted off. It was around 6.30am the next morning that we were awoken with the deafening sound of roaring engines and the sound of gunfire.

Bob, forever the pilot at heart, had recordings and actual film of the Battle of Britain and thought we might enjoy sharing his hobby pre-breakfast. It shook the house. The sausage dog had wheeled itself into a hole and we were shaking like jellies.

"Breakfast anyone?" came the cry as Bob entered in a floral skirt and a blouse that drooped over his floppy gut as if it had no right to be there. Breakfast was a large orange juice with enough vodka in it to eliminate a species. And cornflakes. In between spurts, Bob had informed us the previous night that he'd had some plastic surgery here and there and not to worry, it made him feel good.

All was fine. The morning caaaaaktail had not set in yet and the conversation was flowing about George C. Scott.

As he slurped his juice and attacked his cornflakes, I became aware that all was not well with the contours on his face. As he rabbited away and took a mouthful, there came an almighty plop as one by one, two bits of plastic fell from holes in his cheeks into his cereal bowl.

As I stared on disbelievingly, Catherine just continued chatting.

She was used to Bob. I certainly wasn't.

We were meant to stay for three days. After making excuses about having to get back to town, we departed. I can recall now, as if it was yesterday, the unbridled joy and sheer elation of jumping in the Volkswagen and heading for home.

Bob would later pass on to the great cross dresser in the sky – bless him. It must have a been a very unhappy life, but jeez – what a nutter!

Catherine's grandparents, Mimi and Ricky, were as bizarre but infinitely more loveable. Both in their 70s, they were Hollywood in a box! She claimed to have invented Scrabble and showed me the original mock-up she had hidden in the wardrobe. He was an ex-mobster who'd done the Vegas route and beyond. He was a sparkling man, ghost white hair and razor-sharp suits, while she looked like a stylish mix of Betty Grable and Barbara Stanwyck in their heydays. Both utterly amazing people who welcomed me into the flock as a sheepdog to the lamb.

Catherine's son, Damian, was a complete and utter joy. Not only was he Denny Laine's son, but he was his bloody double. We got on great and still do. He was obsessed with Asian girls and in fact would only date them. He'd met the lovely Anna and their resulting son, John, was another joy to behold.

Damian had been so named, after a suggestion by Richard Harris that he was named after his own son, which didn't surprise me at all.

I've always thought that the old adage, 'Two nations divided by the same language,' really did appertain to the UK and USA. And, indeed, just because two nations' peoples looked similar, there couldn't be two more different types of people on the planet.

Deep down, Catherine, still thought I'd leave her one day and end up with the devil incarnate, a certain... Maggie.

Catherine had the foresight and intuition of a Fairy Godmother, and however hard I tried, I couldn't get her to budge in that belief. Even though we were in love – she still carried that with her each and every day.

As the auditions came and went, and went, so the near misses continued to come with worrying rapidity. Nearly getting a huge part in Mike Myers' *So I married An Axe Murderer* as a pilot, down to a fourth 'call back' and then – nothing.

It always seemed to be just around the corner! My consistent refusal to take acting class was taking its toll, but I was adamant. I was a seasoned performer and I didn't need it. Deep inside I was petrified to stray from my comfort zone – even though I knew it was screwing up my chances of a real Hollywood career.

By the late summer of '93 money continued to be as rare as rocking horse shit. Somehow, we were surviving. My parents would send 'red cross' parcels full of Branston Pickle, Coleman's Mustard, and pound notes. Reports back from the UK were not good. The Holland Park mansion was now in shreds – rot had been found in the still empty flat and plans were afoot to tear the bugger down and rebuild! I had still somehow been paying the mortgage, and looking back it shows what a total twat I was as it lay empty all those years gathering dust. And dry rot! But still, I hung on to the fact that things would happen and I could reclaim it in a frantic flossy and frenetic return home stuffed to the gills with dollar bills and more money than cents.

CHAPTER 50

Lost for Words?

I knew of Randy Randall Rudy Quaid through his memorable performances in *The Last Detail* and *Midnight Express*, a fine actor and comedian, with a more famous brother, Dennis, but a 'real' Hollywood stalwart in every sense of the word. I collected the 'sides' from the agency lot, late one Friday, and excitedly ran through my 10 lines.

I was up for the role of Game Show Host on Quaid's newbie, a sci-fi comedy called *Martians go Home*.

This, in fact, was a torrid affair with several well-known Hollywood stand-ups painted bright green and pretending to invade Earth. Even on paper it looked total shite, and what Quaid was doing in it, fuck knows!

There's an old music hall gag about a budding actor who gets a break in an 'off Broadway' take of Shakespeare's Hamlet. He has five lines and is determined that this is his big break. For weeks he strides around, "Hark I hear a cannon," is his one line. All he has to do is to wait until a cannon goes off on the ramparts above and utter those immortal words. For weeks he bores his wife to death relating the words over and over again. "Hark I hear a cannon - HARK I HEAR a cannon!" And so it goes until the opening night. As the mists clear, the cannon sounds a huge blast... BOOM! Reeling around the actor cries out, "What the hell was that?"

And so, I had a week till the audition with Randy himself and an old lady who was playing the game show contestant. I had a few more lines than Mr Hamlet, twelve in fact! My first line was to the contestant... "And welcome to you and good luck, Mrs Worthington." I too spent the following week hoofing around town, washing up, in the bath, lying in bed, repeatedly cranking out the line time after time after time.

On the day of the audition, I looked the part, glasses, neat suit, flashy tie - the works.

Although I was very used to the TV 'set', there's something about a Hollywood stage that daunts and defies one's experience. I was indeed a virgin veteran. Shaken and stirred.

So, it began.

"And welcome to you and good luck Mrs Worthington," I mumbled to myself as the air-con clanked shut and the lights began to glare.

"ACTION, Steve!"

I think you know what's coming, and in truth, I think I did too as I stared into the huge lens. "And a very good evening to... erm...

"CUUUUUUUT," came the cry from the director. "Thats OK, now let's go again, and this time, let's nail the lines, Steve."

"ACTSHUNNNN."

"Hello, Mrs Worthington," I mumbled. I could see my portly co-star reel in despair. And so it went. Eight takes later - could I get the words out? Could I bollocks!

Where's ones autocue when one needs it!

Stricken – shattered - shitting myself, I was led away to my dressing room. I sat crying like a baby. This was IT. I was bombing like an air raid. Once more my mind was full of Trish and the others shouting at me to take 'class'.

A knock on the door and there stood Quaid. "It's okay, my friend. We all get this at some stage," he said, as he put his huge arms around me. "Take a minute, then let's go again. Okay?"

And that I did. After around twenty takes, I'd completed my scene. The portly lady huffed and departed, then Quaid and a few of the comics came up and gave me the Tinseltown hug and the customary clap. I ran from the set as if my arse was on fire and, without thinking, headed straight for the one place I felt safe, the Formosa, where Lindy obligingly fixed me several of his earth-shaker martinis. But I was in pieces. Yet again, I'd let Trish down. I felt like getting on that plane and getting my arse back to blighty.

I was a dizzy, demented mess. Head in hands I heard a voice, "Hey, you okay?" It was Trish. She'd tracked me down and was now holding me tight. I felt as if my world had caved in. All that work. Yet when it came to it, I couldn't crack it.

No autocue, no Blacknell!

In the end the film didn't amount to much, in fact Catherine and I went to the opening, and closing, of said masterpiece at a movie theatre just off Hollywood Boulevard. There were four people in the cinema, Catherine, myself, the projectionist and a cleaner. At least they got my name right in the credits.

One of the rare truisms Bob told me once was, “Stephen, in Hollywood, NEVER, ever, be 40! It’s the kiss of fucking death!” At that stage I didn’t know whether I could face being forty in Hollywood anyway.

CHAPTER 51

Tea-Time With Tim

"Tim's coming for tea," Catherine piped one bright and sunny LA Monday morning.

Tim?" I said, "Tim who?"

"You'll know him when you see him," she smiled.

After several hours cleaning the apartment, fluffing up pillows and spraying enough smelly stuff around to fell an elephant, she sat me down and said, "Whatever you see and hear - this is just between us. It's private, okay? And did you get the Guinness?"

Who was it? Hitler? Clark Gable? Ginger Rogers? My mind was whizzing as I heard a faint whistle through the open windows. As it grew louder so Catherine's eyes grew bigger, until, a knock on the door and, as I tentatively opened it, there was a white faced, tartan suited, long-haired man with a big black doctor's bag.

"Is Miss Catherine at home?" it uttered. "Why, of course, please come in," I stuttered.

As they embraced it was clear they were old friends and that, at least, was a comfort as it felt that PT Barnum's circus had popped in for a cuppa! It then sort-of dawned on me who I had in my sitting room.

Herbert Butros Khaury, alias Dary Dover... alias Sir Timothy Timms - alias Larry Love, the Singing Canary - alias - TINY TIM.

He was there - sitting on my couch.

"Nice to meet you, Mr Stephen," he said in his shrill falsetto voice as he lifted a six-pack of Guinness and a well-worn looking banjo from the mysterious black bag. Without a word, he started to play, and play he did. He played for almost two and half hours non-stop. The entire history of rock and roll from *A Bicycle Built for Two* and *Shine on Harvest Moon* to *You Are My Sunshine, Making Whoopee* and *Blueberry Hill* to *Heartbreak Hotel* and *We'll Meet again.* He'd already achieved a world record in '88 with a century of song in one smash hit with the *'World Professional Non-stop Singing record'*. And it appeared we were getting another crack at it. It was indescribable, all the time sipping Guinness as if that was the last drop he'd ever take. Once he'd dried out, I was dispatched to get the other six pack from the kitchen. But warm, never cold, that's how Tim liked it.

As the clock struck seven, Tim arose and with a sprawling hug trailed out of the door, whistling as he went. I was flabbergasted.

I'd had a picture of the *'Tiptoe Through the Tulips'* on that infernal wall, and I'd just had tea and Guinness with 'im!

Tim was to pass away a few years later, leaving the term 'one-off' as his and his alone. I have never ever forgotten it. I did realise there and then that Mrs B did have a past, and an amazing one too. That day it dawned on me… I was living a dream. A small one, but a dream no less.

All the women I'd ever loved were all so amazing and now dear Catherine had proved once more to be another cup of Tinseltown tea altogether.

CHAPTER 52

A Load Of Cock and Ball

To get any work in Hollywood at all was a cause for celebration. Such was the overwhelming competition within that tight knit community.

So, when I heard that the dreaded Playboy TV channel was looking for a professional TV 'host' I was on it quicker than a cheetah on roller skates.

The show in question was *'The Love and Sex Test'* which was really an excuse to talk about willies and pubic hair.

I sailed through the auditions, and they were more than happy with my British accent – although I did need to roll my RRRR's and call myself Steve Black-NELL.

It was all done in a small studio not three or five miles from our house, and the pay was amazingly good for a nice change.

It was a crude and simple format. Basically, I would present three scenarios and only one was true.

Each filmed segment had a voice over explaining the usually preposterous idea, i.e. Pubic hair wigs for animals – and only one of the three proposed was true.

I'm sure there was a local magician as my co-host – but my main memory is that we all called the show 'A Thousand Ways to Say Penis'!

It was literally a load of bollocks – but huge fun to do.

I can only recall thinking what my BBC chums at home would have thought of it, but it was work, and THAT was what I was there for.

Despite this seemingly vast array of superstars popping up all over the place, Hollywood is, in fact, just like any other town in the USA, it's just flatter, dirtier and more dangerous than so many of its counterparts.

Each night I'd walk home from the store, up the ten blocks or so to La Brea towards the hills and to our little house. Then the next day I'd read that there had been so many muggings and so many murders in the same area. I was lucky to say the very least. And you had to watch where you strayed too!

CHAPTER 53

Danger In Paradise and Bye Bye Ken

One night I decided to walk a different route home and instead of turning right out of the store to walk up La Brea to the hills, I turned to go north up Highland. I was only a few hundred yards further when I heard a loud shriek and before I knew it, I was being pelted with stones and tin cans. With true British resolve I decided to get the hell out of there and was pursued by a gang of what looked like kids until I did a dramatic left on to the relative safety of Sunset Blvd.

Perhaps the one time that it all really hit me just how far from home I actually was, was the day when CNN reported rumblings afoot in Downtown LA, which turned into full-on riots.

After going through thin and thinner times, I was actually pretty happy. Catherine and I had a sedate and happy existence.

Despite having Maurice White from Earth Wind Fire round for tea and bikkies, getting so close to global fame, and working for a nano-second with so many great names, my old flat mate, Ken had tired of it all and naffed off back to the UK.

We'd been through so much and we both knew that, really, we'd failed, but felt proud of giving it a go. I went to see him off at the apartment block and while he was bidding his goodbyes to his chums, I felt a familiar urge, and it was three days later that I got a call. "Thanks for the three potatoes and that carrot in my luggage, Babe. Love ya Babe."

I was getting rumblings from home about my mansion flat! It was still lying empty, and my UK funds had run out, so selling it seemed the only way out. The thought of more than a few grand winging its way across the water into what was left of my Californian account filled me with a new hope and vigour that had been sadly lacking.

Then came the call from my sister. With the dry rot in the whole block, it was all a disaster site. After two months of back and forth, here and there, I agreed to the sale. It worked out that after everything was paid - mortgage arrears, repairs and a zillion other stupid things, I received the princely sum of £1,500! I'd bought it for £140,000 and it should have shot up in value. A great plan except that idiot features here was so up his rectum he screwed everything up well and truly. Big Nose Blacknell strikes again!!

CHAPTER 54

Bonked To Blighty and Back

Rumblings were being felt in the marriage too. The lack of money and success was taking its toll, and I decided maybe a trip home for a few weeks might bring the 'missability' factor into play. Trying to run a love nest in a town with no heart was proving all too much and we knew we needed a break.

I had long adhered to the adage that no flight was a flight unless you were pissed.

My choice of cloud cocktail was a bloody Mary. I'd always have one or two at the airport, then grab a half bottle of vodka to top up the free mini ones on board with generous glugs into the plastic glass and off you jolly well went! I've never been a nervous flyer, but had always loved dropping pills down my gullet. It was a hangover from my nursing and hippy days, plus the fact that I'm an addictive son of a bitch.

"Whatever you do Stephen," Catherine said that morning, "Only take one of these... and keep the others for emergencies." As the cab made its way down the seemingly endless La Brea, that would more or less take me straight to LAX, my mind was overflowing with strange and diverse thoughts.

Where was home? Was it really back in the UK or would I be giving everything up to leave this weird and wonderful place? As I entered the ticket lounge, I gleefully popped one of the little white buggers and headed for the bar. Three large BM's later, I felt suitably equipped, and only dallying to pick up a quart of vodka, I slinked on board. Oh, those were days when it was all so easy to smuggle shit.

Hunched in my fifth-class economy seat at the back of the plane, I was feeling rather perky with the excitement of it all. So, without flinching threw down the other two pills with a massive glug of British Airways vodka and Mr T Bloody Mary mix topped up with enough vodka to stir a nun's promise.

"Are you okay, son?" came a voice through the mist, "We were worried about you."

As my eyes blearily opened like a rusty drawbridge, I could just make out the shape of my father's face, peering over me. Then Mum came into vision...

"Hello Stephen?"

It transpired that the unique and devilish combo of the wife's pills and a crate of vodka had caused me to collapse on to the gangway off the plane. I had been stretchered off and put in a quiet room, while an attendant went to the greeting bit to see if they could find my dad who was picking me up. He'd heard it on the tannoy and had wheeled me to his car and driven me back to their home in Stubbington, Hampshire, which was where I eventually woke up.

Through the years, my parents had seen many a sight and lived through a world war, so they took it all rather calmly. Looking back, it was a daft thing to do, but then I was very daft.

Nothing changes I suppose.

Seeing everyone again and spending time with Maggie was a joy.

Catherine and Maggie had in fact met on an abortive trip we'd made nine months earlier – and swords were drawn - hence my wife immediately becoming convinced that I would end up back with her!

This to me seemed preposterous. Meanwhile Maggie was still with that dodgy bloke who had a habit of popping up everywhere she and I went! Jealous? Just a bit!

It turned out he too had the same idea about Maggie and I getting back together which, again, to her was crazy. We both adored our partners, so why the hell we would even consider going back in time to rekindle a romance of some two decades before? It seemed to be a forlorn fantasy of monolithic proportions.

On landing back at LAX, I felt a distinct lack of excitement. The buzz wasn't there. The same when I reconvened with Mrs B. Looking back, I think, maybe, we both knew something was up, but we resumed life as we knew it and just carried on as normal, whatever that was.

The UK trip had taken just about all my money. One fine Monday, I found myself outside the bank on Hollywood Blvd staring at the hole in the wall. My balance, it declared was $42 on the nose.

The mansion money had all been used up and the tramps sitting on the sidewalk had more in their begging cups.

But at least I had another audition that day, so, I parked up on Sunset and marched in, perky and smart - American accent and big nose in place. Maybe THIS was it. It was a national ad for breakfast cereal - a huge earner! With the down and outs begging just yards away from the Hollywood Walk of Fame, a place where the rich and poor mix silently together, I figured, maybe, I was meant to get this one.

Having delivered my silly self and, to my mind, impressed the shit out of them, I breezed out onto the street. As I neared what was left of my car, I noticed a yellow ticket on the windscreen. A fine of $40 dollars for exceeding the time limit. I gazed up at the sun. Distant memories filled my head. Tramp nightclub, MTV, Live Aid, the chauffeur, the drugs, the mansion flat - and now this. I had two dollars IN THE WORLD!

It all suddenly hit me. I'd really screwed this up big time. Tears rolled down my cheeks as those voices that you see in the movies came and went inside my head.

Two dollars. I was worth a mere two dollars.

From 1983-85 I had been earning around £300k plus a year!

I now felt diminished... down and very, very out. I'll never forget poor Catherine's face when I got home with the news. It's a feeling I'll never forget.

I thought of the old balloon gag. The daddy balloon says to everyone... "You've let yourselves down and worst of all you've let me down." It would have been funny if it hadn't been so true.

A week later as I was pootling up the freeway towards the infamous Downtown, where LA was born way back in 1781 – when I heard a clanking and realised that the mudguard had become detached from the rear and was grinding along the tarmac. I was pulled over by the cops and ticked off. That was the beginning of the end of the Blacknell transport. I sold it for parts for next to sod all.

All this time my mum and dad had been writing and calling and, of course, it was my job to say that everything was going great... Catherine was great, the dog was great, I was great - everything was GREAT. But deep down I knew that things were looking a trifle desperado!

If ever a place on Earth was transitional, then Hollywood epitomises that to a tee.

One of my musical hero's was the genial oddball that was Kevin Ayres, he of Soft Machine fame, who made some great albums. One of my favourite lines of his was 'I can count my friends on one finger' and this felt so, so apt for the way I was starting to feel.

When I thought back to the welcoming party Ken and I had at the Sunset Apartment, it had been seething with new people, all eager to be part of the new adventure. Minus wheels, as I plodded home along the scorched sidewalk, those words dropped into my head.

After years in town, how many friends did I actually have? It came to me, Trish, Alan, my wonderful silly chum, Tobbe - and that was it.

There was Catherine of course, but I think we could both feel things were not right. I'd surely have given up the movie dream long before, but the marriage had given me a reason to be there.

With that starting to crumble, my thoughts were continually turning back to the UK.

Although it was frowned upon by wifey, I was still in regular touch with Maggie. Catherine was still consumed by the idea that Maggie and I would get back together. From what I could gather, Maggie's bloke was banging on about it all the time too.

Indeed, it felt that maybe, just maybe, my Tinseltown adventure might be at an end.

"I'm getting married!" shouted my sister, Claire, down the phone early one Sunday morning.

"Can you come home for it?" She sounded so happy, and with Dad promising to send me the flight money, well what could I say?

"If you go, you won't come back," whispered Catherine.

"OF COURSE I WILL," I snapped. "My life is here - with you and Gabby, don't be so stupid."

Gabby the Yorkie and I had become inseparable. She seemed happy as could be stuffed in my coat or trailing after me on long afternoon walks through the hills. I had been close to pets before, but this little bundle of furry joy was life itself.

One typically bright Hollywood Sunday afternoon, I was summoned from my usual rooftop radio spot by Catherine screaming, “Steve, come quick Gabriella's not well. HURRY!”'

The little one was fast asleep in her basket. But that appeared to be the problem as she'd been there since 7am. Even her favourite treats waved under her little wet nose had failed to arouse her. We were both beside ourselves in panic.

A visit to the vet, that we couldn’t afford, later, it was confirmed that our Gabby had got pregnant! Just how, we couldn’t figure – but the fact was, she was! Perhaps it had been that cute little pug in the next street. But Gabby was going to be a mum!

After some weeks, which felt like many months, the day was upon us. We'd sought good advice and were more than ready if anything went wrong.

Around three in the morning we heard some very strange sounds coming from the lounge, but we were not at all prepared for what we were about to see. There, laying at the side of a very ruffled and sweaty Gabriella were five cute little pups, all black and tan and a delight for the eyes.

As I drew closer my throat seized, and my heart sank. I realised that neatly nestled together in a huddle, four of them were dead. It was the saddest thing I ever witnessed. As a nurse I had become used to bodies, I was a hard nut. But burying them in the smallest grave in the front garden was one of the worst moments of my life.

The lone pup was never named, as one of Catherine’s chums was looking for a new addition and he joined her eight weeks later.

I'd now informed my erstwhile darling agents that I'd be away again for 8 - 10 days. I'd not been the golden boy of such promise, and the auditions had been drying up a tad. Maybe I was now knock, knock, knocking at those same doors!

Catherine insisted that the next trip was going to end our marriage. Whether it was pure paranoia on her part or just a lack of self-esteem, I couldn’t figure it out. But there was no money for two flights – so it was a bicycle trip for one!

CHAPTER 55

Hello Again Green and Pleasant

On Tuesday, June 17th, 1992, I found myself once more in the charming little hamlet of Stubbington in Hampshire, deep in the heart of the English countryside.

I had made it. Now free of the dreaded jet lag, I felt relaxed and happy to be at my dear Sis's wedding. That day, I felt alive and lucky to be there. My parents looked in great nick and all was good with the world.

As I customarily slugged back the free champers, my mind kept drifting back to my own big day in Hollywood, when I was the happiest man in the world.

Pictures flickered in my head like an old movie. How had it all gone so fucking pear shaped? Was it all HER fault? Was I to blame?

Backstage, the thoughts battled as I chatted away on automatic pilot.

"How was it all going?" people asked. While there's me like a twit telling them how great it was.

We'd been so happy. I was set on the road to true superstardom. It was all so real. I was indeed destined to be the next Steve Blacknell! But ultimately, I'd screwed it all up. I DESERVED to fail. What a plonker!

Despite Catherine's protestations that I would never return, I'd felt that I'd prove her wrong and run back to the hills.

But, there and then, surrounded by my lovely family and things so familiar, it began to feel that the big dream was certainly and most definitely OVER!

Sitting in my folks' lounge sipping coffee a few days later, I was going through in minute detail what had transpired between Mrs B and me. It was not the magnificent tale I was sure I'd tell them one day. I had to admit that, like so many Tinseltown alliances, my marriage had been success-led. Failure could only spell more failure.

Catherine James was many things. Aside from being an undeniable beauty, she was charming and gentle but above all that, she had incredible insight.

It took me three days to write my goodbye letter.

My life was now in total ruins.

I'd left for Hollywood with my head high and so full of it.

My mansion flat with my huge round bed and my even bigger ego were now long gone, and I couldn't even afford a pot to piddle in.

Dear Mum, Dad and Sis - eternally supportive, ever loving, always there! For a month I plunked down in the caravan in the front garden. My tail was now so far up my arse it was sticking out of my nose. There I sat, day in, day out, calling all the people I'd deserted to see if anyone had anything I could do - present that, voice this, front that, but, NOWT. SOD ALL. Zilch.

I left messages for a whole slew of celeb chums, but the silence was deafening.

There were a few old music biz pals that came up trumps though.

Malcolm Hill, a bearded wonder of a man, was still at EMI Records. Malc, along with so many others had been plugging the life out of me when I'd been on t'telly, but now here I was - making empty trips to London in the hope of bumping into someone, anyone who might have a paying gig for me.

I'll never, EVER forget Malcolm shouting down the phone one grey Stubbington day, "Come on into town, Blackers. I'll buy you lunch." I still recall the excitement of that Italian meal and obligatory pond of white wine. "Don't you worry, matey, we'll find something for you."

And he did. Although it was a huge bring down, the pure thrill of actually working again, doing the warm-ups at a Smash Hits concert at Wembley was at least something.

Seventy pounds I got - a princely sum indeed, but as I tried to get myself heard over the sound check and crowd hubbub it dawned on me that I had a long, long way to go. I was back at base camp with a mountain to climb. But that day meant so much to me. Malcolm Hill. I'll never forget it mate.

The late, great music publisher/music mogul/pious bullshitter and all-round amazing bloke, Tim Hollier, had been a 60s hippy mini-phenomenon. A man who never cracked the big time but had made a delightful dent in the music of the day.

He had now morphed into a powerful business-man. Always doing the deal, always making a pile of dollars. We had hung out in Hollywood, every meal, every drink, it was ALL down to him. Tim talked 24/7 and would take the wheel at each and every event he attended, being an expert on every subject known to man, woman, and beast. But underneath all the bullshit, he was a mountain of love and human kindness.

He lived in a first floor flat in West Kensington with his second wife, Vivvy, a beautiful lady outside and in, who painted and designed stuff for a living. She was an angel. And there was their teenage son, Rupert, a spiritual dynamo who spent a lot of time in India trying to find himself.

I now had £50 in the bank. The sedentary Stubbington life was, to be honest, driving me nuts, although Mum and Dad and Claire were a never-ending source of encouragement and optimism.

"Come and live with us!" piped Tim, on one of our frequent marathon calls. "We'll charge you fuck all too!!" This was the veritable gift from heaven. Rupert was away on a spiritual sojourn, so within two short days I had moved into his room with a case full of clothes, and blessings from my lovely and exceedingly relieved family.

My days were spent chatting with the lovely Vivvy on how to correct the planet's problems over a glass of wine or ten.

I soon discovered Maggie was living in trendy downtown Tooting with her daft musician chum and ex-lover John McBurnie, a highly talented musician and a very silly man who'd played with Kiki Dee, Camel, and everyone else!

The contents of John's fridge were simply Tofu and Vodka. Maggie had tried to cook his meals, but he was dedicated to becoming a healthy addict of sorts. I called her and we decided to meet. It was a Saturday morning, and we'd agreed I'd go over to her place.

"Here you go young Steve. Here's a tenner to get some wine and pay for the tube fare," said Tim that grey October Saturday morning. It brought tears to my eyes and still, to this day, it's the biggest ten pounds I've ever had in my sweaty little pocket. Bless you Tim. We all miss you.

I'd started divorce proceedings to dear Catherine and to her eternal credit, she had been a complete star with it all. It wasn't easy, I guess, suddenly not having your husband around, leaving an empty apartment to contend with. But divorced we were, by post, in Croydon Crown Court no less.

She'd been correct and all seeing to the very end. Bless her.

But aside from failing magnificently in Hollywood, I'd felt hemmed in by the marriage too. Catherine was and remains such a lovely person, but with both our partners forcing us back together – there really wasn't much hope.

Of course, Gabby was to be left behind, as was Sooty, my beloved puppet. He had been left behind with Catherine on the understanding that I'd have to go back to Hollywood to get him. But there he stayed.

I'd been so close to that little doggie, and when would I see that lovely bit of old cloth again? Was I to be forever Sooty-less?

Seeing Maggie again was a nerve tingling experience. Was Catherine correct that we would fly into each other's arms?

Well, we did, and she was. It was like I'd never been away.

Just one slight hitch, she was still with that nutty bloke.

As time went on, we would see each other more and more, but he would always appear like a jumping jack-in-the-box. Possessive to the nth degree.

The final word from the now ex-Mrs B came one Monday morning with a knock at the door. It was the post with a somewhat battered cardboard box. Postmark USA! As I fumbled to get it undone, there, peeping out of the tissue paper with his one good eye was Sooty!

Catherine was – and is - no ordinary person – and this was an extraordinary thing to do.

With that I felt the umbilical link with Hollywood had been finally severed.

CHAPTER 56

Home Again

I continued to see Maggie and slowly, very slowly, we both imagined us getting together once more. She was shocked though at how I'd changed. Gone was the red-haired, C-minus celeb, loudmouthed rich kid. Instead, this normally overly-shy girl was having to cover for me in company.

My nerves were shot. I found it almost impossible to communicate in a crowd and I felt like the bad actor that I was, calling for a stateside 'prompt' every few minutes so I could continue a chat. It was a complete turnaround.

Hollywood had unknowingly stripped me of 'the party doesn't start without me' feeling. In fact, I didn't even feel I should be invited!

Amid all this, I was still struggling to find real work, and by chance, I bumped into me old drinky mate, little Willy White. He had been married to Spike Milligan's daughter, Silee, so we went back quite a few years. He was now married to another lovely lady, Lori, who was a well-respected magazine editor with the H. Bauer Group, and they had a very nice house in groovy downtown Putney.

Will invited me to din dins.

I must admit I felt like a teeny-weeny fish in a vast empty ocean. All my big nosed bravado had disappeared, and in its place a hesitant, uncertain tremble of a man with little or no direction, no life to speak of, no wife to speak of and a future that offered nothing. I was old news with nowhere to go!

"What about doing some showbiz for us?" said Lori. "EH? What me?" I spat my Chardonnay across the table.

"Yes, why not," she said, "You lived there, you know the buzz on what's hot etc. You can do a weekly thingy for TV Quick."

Within a few weeks, I was ensconced as a fully paid Hollywood correspondent.

Even though I didn't get a credit, and who the fuck was I anyhooooow? I still loved it, and it proved to be my first rung back on the ladder of professional life.

The money was fair, and I worked my little Blacknell socks off to keep the standard of Tinseltown bollocks to my editor's full satisfaction!

Just like Catherine, Maggie's partner had retreated to the ramparts and could see Maggie and I gradually falling in love again.

Countless times she'd say, "Not yet, I'm not ready."

After a night out, I'd see her safely on the tube – and run alongside – waving frantically until the tunnel got in the way.

It hurt so very bad. For indeed, I'd gone head over heels once more for my brown eyed beauty. The familiar old feelings were coming right back at me.

She was now working for the mighty Mike Corby. An ex-Olympian, he ran the 'Fitness Exchange' clubs sited all over London with a rod of brass. A man of great intensity, he treated Maggie well, and, most nights in the week, I'd meet her in the bar there and talk bollocks. The world at large - and us.

"He's gone," she said, over a double large gin and tonic one sweaty August evening. Unbridled joy was followed by the same, then some more.

Of course, we'd have to take it verrrry gently and not wade in. Well, that was fine by me. I'd wait till the moon turned blue. It was as if the world had turned full circle and I was sitting in the sun again. I was blessed.

Things were now rolling along with my career too. TV Quick had given me great confidence, and I'd picked up the lovely gig of working with me old mucker, the late Steve Wright, on BBC Radio 2 as his 'Movie Man'. I felt things were coming together again.

By the summer of 1993, I'd gone into business with my great chum, the ever eccentric 'pink lady', Frizzby Fox, and the fearlessly funny, Mr Gideon Wagner.

The Limelight Club was an 80's Goth/pretentious project designed to bring in the London trendies. Although we had high hopes, it was doomed from the start because... well, it was a crap idea. But a week before it closed, I had a visit from one Belinda Chandler. She had heard about me.

She headed up the entertainment at 'In Flight Productions' and, there and then, offered me the job of fronting not only

Virgin's first ever 'In flight' TV show, but to come on board as the Cathay Pacific host. That's the man you saw leaping about like a twat on the screen as you sped to your glamorous destinations.

The money was amazing - £1000 per global trip!

It was brilliant. Picked up by cab, first class flight to Hawaii, LA, NYC, Canberra etc. the world was my handbag. Quick flight, drinks on board – hotel – drinks next day on a beach or whatever, fuck my six lines up, then drinks, bed and flight home.

Lots of drinks! What a gig! I was on me way back!

I was now firmly back on my tootsies, and having scraped enough money, I started to look around for a place to live.

'Cottage For Sale' it read. 'Secluded spot in Shepherd's Bush area of West London.' Cottage? Yesssss! It was like Cornwall all over again!!

I bought it. It was wondrous... lonely, but pretty fucking cool.

My dad, bless him, came and stayed for a week to help me paint the entire thing in Lincoln Green; Floors, walls, ceilings, the lot. He said it was daft as I'd never sell it. The very thought!

And then there was Maggie. My head and heart were finally in alliance.

I had a choice to make. Single, silly, irresponsible, lonely, and a puppet for a companion, drooling over my memories of failed auditions and past failures, or life with my ever-tolerant and forgiving Maggie.

I did sell the cottage, and it was during a trial spell together in her Crystal Palace flat that we knew we were back in love.

I had my Maggie back!

CHAPTER 57

Beside The Seaside

In 2007 we moved to Hythe, one of Kent's magnificent Cinque ports, to a beautiful house overlooking the sea. We nicknamed it Carnaby Heights!

Maggie had been working on check-out at the local Waitrose, but started to feel that something was very wrong. She was diagnosed with breast cancer in December of 2021. It was terrible, terrible news.

A course of intense and gruelling chemotherapy followed and, glad to say, praise be to Buddha, that she was declared cancer free in the Spring of 2025, and we are now looking to spending our remaining days with our two cats in the yard – and all the fun of the seaside.

It only occurred to me recently that the lyric in the A Flock of Seagulls' hit '*I Ran*' which affected me so much goes... With auburn hair and tawny eyes – the kind of eyes that hypnotize me through...

Well, that explains my early love life!

But I'm so lucky to have finally settled with my wonderful Maggie.

As the Buddhists say, 'You're only here three billion times so you'd better enjoy yourself'. All I can hope is that each time I'm here, I get to have a bedroom wall so I can have fun all over again.

And my wall? Well – it's long gone now, I'm sure – but I'll never, ever forget how an innocent carefree teenager managed to meet so many of his heroes.

WHAT a privilege!

Postscript

I love my life as a self-unemployed and very often 'free' lance' whatever it is that I do.

After eighteen years, I still run London's premiere 'media networking' club, *The Waffle,* which has gone from strength to strength... and indeed still PR rock and roll acts, as well as being a volunteer for Age UK. I have even managed to cram in a 'Top of the Pops' Anniversary book with my long-time cohort Mr Patrick Humphries.

After those seminal years of trying to 'make it', and despite overwhelming spates of stupidity, selfish behaviour and unfortunate addictions – I count myself as a lucky lad for having good friends and family that have stuck by me along this forever rocky road.

Despite losing all that money and ignoring those who knew best for me – I find myself relatively at peace.

As I reflect, I know that nothing will EVER replace the wonderful people who've passed through my life and been so essential along my journey. I'd give anything and everything to have Mum and Dad back by my side, life without them is just not the same. They supported me through every silly, ridiculous, moment. How I miss them.

I'd also like to thank a few folks for their help and understanding throughout these decades;

My lovely sister Claire.

Catherine for giving me a life in LA.

The mighty Pedro and son, Daz.

Ken Gold for our hilarious times together and Tobbe Hanson being such a good friend amidst the chaos of Tinseltown. And Trish Planck for all her help and guidance.

John Burrowes for believing in me.

Dave Williams for the Heineken.

David Preston, a force of nature.

Ian King OBE – my life's mentor who took me through the Duke of Edinburgh Award Scheme from Bronze to Gold and gave me such inner strength.

Five Elements acupuncture for being there on many occasions.

Patrick Humphries for his never-ending support, knowledge and help with the opening bit.

Will White for all things photographic.

Ms. Bush and her lovely manager.

And thanks to Willy Wymold for the lovely words.

Raechel and David and everyone at The Old Treacle Publishing Partnership for their work in making head or tail of this nonsense.

And, of course, my darling Maggie.

And as the Honeybus classic, *I Can't Let Maggie Go* fades into the distance, I bid you farewell.

Author

Steve Blacknell lives on the Kent coast with his wife, Maggie. He runs a media training company along with the Waffle Club, a networking venue in Covent Garden where the great and good of the arts mingle and waffle about their current and future projects. To contact Steve Blacknell with any comments, insults or promises of money, please email teeheesb@yahoo.com.

To contact Old Treacle Press Ltd.

info@oldtreaclepartnership.com

For information on Old Treacle Press

www.oldtreaclepartnership.com

2025

Printed in Great Britain
by Amazon

6ad0182e-09bc-47e9-9067-0d2547ac4102R01